Clouds Pile Up in the North

New & Selected Poems

Clouds Pile Up in the North

New & Selected Poems

Maj Ragain

Press 53
Winston-Salem

Press 53, LLC
PO Box 30314
Winston-Salem, NC 27130

First Edition

The Silver Concho Poety Series
edited by Pamela Uschuk and William Pitt Root

Cover design by Kevin Morgan Watson

Cover art, "Worker Ants: The Clouds Pile Up,"
12" x 12" oil on panel,
Copyright © 2016 by Jessica Damen,
photographed by Norman Watkins,
used by permission of the artist.

Author photo by John Reeves
Cover artist photo by Vickie Gray

Library of Congress Control Number: 2017954779

Printed on acid-free paper
ISBN 978-1-941209-68-4

This book is dedicated to Bill Root and Pamela Uschuk,
who shepherded it from the beginning and kept wind in my sails

To my wife LuAnn, her patience, love and kindness

To my children, Sean and Megan; may the years be kind to them

Some of the poems in this collection were previously published in the following journals and anthologies:

'To My Son, From Greece," and "Walking in the Bamboo," *Fresh Oil Loose Gravel*, Burning Press, editor Luigi Bob Drake, Lakewood, Ohio, 1996

"A Small Winter Meditation for the Humped," and "Sleepless with Mussolini," *Burley One Dark Sucker Fired*, Maj Ragain, editor Larry Smith, Bottom Dog Press, 1998

"For My Daughter Meg, Graduating from Kent Roosevelt High School," *A Hungry Ghost Surrenders His Tackle Box*, Maj Ragain, Bottom Dog Press, editor Larry Smith, 2006

"Under the Guidance of Falling Petals," *After the Bell*, edited by Anderson & Hassler, University of Iowa Press, Iowa City, Iowa, 2007

"Willows," *Come Together/Imagine Peace*, edited by Metres, Smith & Smith, Harmony Series, Bottom Dog Press, Huron, Ohio, 2008

"For My Mother Beatrice Summers, on Her 90th Birthday," Broadside, edited by Tom Kryss, Black Rabbit Press, Charlestown, Ohio, 2010. In an edition of 50 copies

"Farm Market," Broadside, Costmary Press, editor Dean Keller, Kent, Ohio 2011

"Letter to America, from Ta Pham Duy Tien," *Traveling Stanzas Project*, Wick Poetry Center, Kent State University, Kent, Ohio, 2015

"Greeting the Poets at an Open Reading, Last Exit Books, Kent, Ohio" *Artful Dodge*, 52 & 53, editor, Dan Bourne, Wooster, Ohio, 2016

"Hammer on the Roof, Morning Meditation," Broadside and Audio, Wick Poetry Center, Kent State University, Kent, Ohio 2017

"The Brief Life of Honeysuckle," *Truth to Power: Writers Respond to the Rhetoric of Hate and Fear*, editor Pamela Uschuk, *Cutthroat, A Journal of the Arts*, 2017

Contents

Introduction: Home to the Sargasso Sea
   by Maj Ragain   xiv

I

Rogue Wave in the Rose Bushes   3
An Old Man Lies Down with the Lion   4
A Haircut in Standing Rock Cemetery   5
The Comet Leaves Us Behind   7
Jawbone Barks at the Annual Weekend Poetry Festival   10
Celebration of the New Mural by Cherokee Artist
   Edwin George   13
Clouds Pile Up in the North   15
A Finger at the Temples   18
A Letter Finds Merle Mollenkopf on His 70th Birthday   21
Conversation with William E. Towers   23
For My Daughter Meg, Graduating from Kent
   Roosevelt High School   24
Business of the Day   25
Doctor Williams' Plumtree   27
East Liverpool Mantra   28
Keeping the Word: The Horseplayer's Creed   29
Poverty, That Flower   30
Living in the Margin   31
These Blues   32

II

Farm Market   37
The Men in the Mountain   38
Find the Poem in the World   41
For Marv Smith: a Farewell   43
Gathered Under the Full Wolf Moon   44
Fancy Gap   47
Sleepless with Mussolini   49
Test the Spirits to See Whether They Are from God   51

A Nest of Stories   52

Words Inked on a Federal Reserve Note   54

A Longing to Be Pure   55

Jawbone Annual Open Poetry Readings/May
     2009, Kent, Ohio   56

Gypsies in the Olive Grove   59

I Wish to Be Warmly Received   62

Walking in the Bamboo   63

Living Room Yoga/Language of the Dog   65

Lambrini, That Flower   67

The Old House in Tremont, Ohio, Has Its Say   68

III

On the Road to Detroit   71

Kickstarting the Poets at Last Exit Books   72

A Small Winter Meditation for the Humped   74

Strip Mining Memory   76

The Maze Walker Meets John Lee Hooker One
     Last Time   79

All the Way to Heaven Is Heaven   85

For My Mother Beatrice Summers on Her 90th
     Birthday   86

Knock Upon Yourself as Upon a Door for the First
     Time   87

Salt   89

Lake Shining   91

The Hat   93

On the Road to Mandalay   95

To My Son, from Greece   97

I Want to Sing an Old, Old Song   101

Letter to America, from Ta Pham Duy Tien   102

Living from Day to Day Is Never What it Seems   103

Stone Song, Dollars in the Jar   104

Name It What You Will   105

The Anguish That Lives Inside Steel   107

The Small Red Ball   108

Those Who Watch Over Our Sleep and Solitude   111

IV

Hammer on the Roof, Morning Meditation 115

Under the Guidance of Falling Petals 116

A Luminous Phenomenon 122

Fishing the Sky Overturned 124

The Bird Is Caught Simply by the Leg 125

We Contain the Light in Which We Live 127

Halim El Dabh, His 90th Birthday 129

The Dancer Moves Toward the Light 130

Pharmacy 131

The Lame Goat Makes His Way to the High Country 132

Willows 133

Jolly Roger 134

Kamikaze, that Divine Wind 135

A Hungry Ghost Surrenders His Tackle Box 136

V

First Call for Poets 141

The Garden Entrusted to Us 143

Fishing with Jim O'Neill 145

The Mark of My Father's Hand 147

Fold Your Dirty Clothes/Build a Paper Boat 149

A Page from This Day 152

The Brief Life of Honeysuckle 153

Groundhog Day Meditation 154

At the Poker Table, at Sea 158

Lament for Stella Gibson 159

I Will Tell You a Mystery 162

Sleeping in Provincetown 163

Counting the Stitches 164

The Heartbeat of Ordinary Things 166

Introduction:
Home to the Sargasso Sea
by Maj Ragain

The Mystery. "Every writer finds a new entrance. . ." The words of Lin-Chi. That initial opening was for me in childhood, as it is so often, when the Mystery quickened, pulsed, and found its way into my small world. One memory overshadows all others. It may well be the birthplace of the poems that follow, the beginning of a long pilgrimage home over the years.

The summer of 1946 on my grandparents' farm in southeastern Illinois. I was six years old. My grandpa Chet and a half dozen neighboring farmers had gathered to clean the well which was brick lined and filled with deep, cold, dark water fed by springs. One man was lowered down, a rope around his waist and shoulders, with a bucket and a corn knife to cut away the roots which had dislodged the bricks and muddied the well. I got as close as I could to watch him disappear into darkness before my father collared me and made me stand behind him. Bucket after bucket of broken brick and tree roots were hauled up by the men. Half an hour went by. Then deep in the well we all heard a terrified shout. *Get me outta here, get me outta here.* They hauled him up. He was shaken to the core. *Something is down there and it's alive.* One man went to the barn for a big fish hook and a ball of twine. He baited it with meat and cast it down into the well. We all awaited a jerk of the line. *I've got him,* said the man quietly. He hauled it up. What came out of that darkness was an eel, about four long feet, thick as a man's arm, held high in the air by the man who hooked it. The eel thrashed with a fury and changed colors even as we watched, its pale body taking on a blue black sheen in the sunlight. How many years since this eel had seen the sun? The catcher man held it high for a long while, a trophy from another world, then dropped it to the grass, put a boot on the back of its head and cut it off with a hoe. The body was thrown to the hogs.

After the work was finished and the concrete slab was moved back over the well, Dad and I stood for a long while, after the others had left, talking about the snake-dragon creature who was so ugly and beautiful. *Where did it come from?* Dad said, *It swam through the rivers underground. It came from the Sargasso Sea.* I had never known there were rivers and lakes beneath us.

The Sargasso Sea is a strange neighborhood, mid Atlantic, a clockwise spinning eddy, a water clock bounded not by shores but by currents, an area 2000 miles in length, 700 miles wide, with Bermuda in its southwest corner. The Sargasso is covered by kelp, often becalmed, regarded by sailors as a place of bewitchment with its legends of ships found drifting and crewless. This is the birth ground for all Atlantic eels. The larva, "glass eels," ride the currents for up to a year before reaching the coast. By this time, they have grown into "elvers," six inches in length. In the spring, the males find a home in the coastal estuaries, whereas the females, for reasons not known, begin a much longer journey that can extend into the upper Midwest, beyond the Mississippi. They are night travelers, midnight ramblers, swimming creeks and rivers, both above and below the earth, even belly walking across rainy back yards. It may be up to twenty years before the urge to return to the Sargasso Sea begins to throb. The signal to return home, to mate, to perish, cannot be denied. The males along the coast look west. The females stir, quicken and make their way to the Atlantic. Together, they strike out for the kelp beds of the Sargasso Sea. Though vast migrations have been observed, no one has ever seen an eel mate and die in the Sargasso.

The body of the eel still thrashes and churns in the ocean of memory, dancing like the condemned at the end of a rope. A life hardly contained by its form. A living beauty like nothing I'd ever seen. Her death colors came from a place deeper than the well. Her journey ended there in Illinois. She never made it home. The Totten farm has been abandoned for half a century. The well is still there, the walls a tangle of roots and broken bricks, but still open all the way to the Sargasso.

In the darkness, something turns.

I

Remember not to leave this world without ceremony,
to look toward the sun after it is gone,
to cry out when there is no one to listen.

Rogue Wave in the Rose Bushes

I told Lu after the rose bush
had snapped back and thorned
her cheek, after she had lost
her silver earring in the flower bed,
after we lay quietly walking the mountains
on the bedroom ceiling,

Let's leave it all behind now,
clean out the bank accounts,
throw the breaker switches, tell the neighbors
come get what you want, the doors are open.
Let's black spray paint *Jesus Loves Me*
all over Mom's I'm-in-the-nursing home-now
1995 cherry Delta Royale Oldsmobile,
run it through the car wash with the windows down,
half a dozen times, you and me riding up front.
Let's get waxed and make a run toward
the moonrise, a notch off full.

Because when it comes, that rogue wave,
we won't have time to babble more than a mouthful
of words, kicking around in the blue light,
streaming silver shards at each other.
Then we'll be swept away.
Into the cold. Then the dark.

This moment, the air is cinnamon,
sandalwood, sweat honeyed,
here on this high ground with you.

An Old Man Lies Down with the Lion

In an old book
of Zen teachings,
I come across a note,
written in my own hand,
twenty-five years ago.

The lion must slay the dragon.
Each scale bears the words,
'Thou shall.' When the dragon
is slain, one is reborn as a child.

I was delivered into this world
with the dragon's egg
nestled in my breast.
I cannot remember the day
it emerged from its shell,
first a peep, later a snarl.
I have felt its hunger
since boyhood.
One midnight it moved its lair
to the lower bitter regions of my soul.
It began to feed on
what I feared and prayed against.
Neither of us knows what it guards or why.

Nights, the dragon climbs my rib ladder
to lay its head against my heart, lulled to sleep
by the drumbeat.
It is prisoner to the heavy coat of mail
which no sword can pierce, prisoner
to the weight of idle years,
the taste of sulphur and ash, the bars of bone.
Its every dream beckons the lion,
the great jaws tearing open the soft underbelly,
releasing the dragon from its troth.

Thou shall lie down with the lion.
Thou shall be reborn as an old man.

A Haircut in Standing Rock Cemetery

My wife and I roll down through the cemetery
to the Cuyahoga river, the paved road
leading to the great council rock standing midstream.
New graves have begun to appear
in the open grassy field, tombstone toadstools,
new dirt. We pass yesterday's grave,
white wicker flower baskets overturned
on the mound, fresh blush of gladiolas.

I lock the wheels on the chair
at the river's edge.
Its clear waters cut around
the base of Standing Rock.
Lu stands behind me and begins to
snip. I close my eyes and I lean into her breasts.
She straightens me up with a firm hand.
Snip. Snip. I wish to be pruned for
the new season. *Hold still,* she says.
The locks of gray find their way to the grass.
I tell her if a witch finds these cuttings of hair,
I'm in trouble.
Do you think there are any witches
around here? I don't know.

Five more minutes and fall arrives.
Lu, let's be quiet and see
if we can feel the earth tilt
at that moment.
At 6:22, the breeze stops as if between breaths.
Then it stirs. It is fall. *Hold still,*
she says. *Just a little more.*

Lu, look at the light on the river
near the rock. It has changed.
What does it make you feel? she asks.

I say this, as if another man inside
me is speaking and I cannot stop him.
I feel that my heart has gone out
into the world and it will not come back.

The Comet Leaves Us Behind

I wake up this morning wondering about the Hale-Bopp comet, where it is now. It has been ten years since it slipped away from our view. I wonder if someone on another earth is pointing up to it right now, speaking wonderment in a strange language that sounds like a piccolo or tap dancing. I miss it, that burning ghost. I won't see it again.

The phone rings, Rik Walden, the poet with the cracked heart, from Raleigh, North Carolina. Rik sent me a poem weeks ago called *Blue Ghost Prayer Wheels*. He wants to know what I think about it. I can't tell him except in a poem I haven't written. Rik is handcuffed to the meat wheel, turning over the fire pit. He is afraid, he tells me, of becoming invisible to himself. He wants to know whether I can still see him. He now shares a house with a seventeen-year-old cat named Shitty. *We love her*, he says. *We had to take her to the vet. She's about done; she lives on kitty downers.* I don't ask why anyone would name a cat Shitty—especially if you loved her. First, the gone, gone beyond going comet, then this old stoned cat who has to live out her life with the name tag Shitty dangling from her scrawny neck. I am stuck with them, caught in the gravitational field in my head.

Add this to my love, no other word for it, for that skin-and-bones old gray mare who, when I met her, was still held captive in a muddy pen the size of my living room, down off Johnson Road here in Kent. I got her name from her owner, a bearded, disgruntled rascal, who was repairing the barbed wire fence one afternoon when I came a courtin'. *Shalimar*, he groused at me. *Her name is Shalimar. She's twenty-six years old.*

It all started one day when I pulled the car over on the shoulder and clucked to her. She looked up and went back to grazing. The next day, I called to her by name and told her mine. Nothing. A half eaten apple tossed over the fence did it. After that, she'd come right up to me. She hadn't been curried in years. Her unclipped hooves made every step hurt. It was her loneliness, how it clung to her, that brought me back. I saw in her what I feel in myself. I began telling her things I could never surrender to anyone else, crazy shit from knee deep in the wound, the arrow arguing with the bow, moonlight quarreling with the river.

Shalimar. After the Shalimar Gardens, built in seventeenth century India as an Abode of Love. A place where the heart can find shelter. She is beautiful, that old horse, though you wouldn't know it by looking at her. Nobody knows much about the nature of beauty and how it moves the heart. Perhaps beauty is what we are naming our feeling rather than what evokes it.

Larry, who owns the horse farm down the road, eventually came to rescue her and turn her out in a big pasture with other horses. Now, when I drive out to find her in that big open field that runs a quarter-mile back to the tree line, Shalimar is still easy to spot, boney old crone, sway backed grandmother, always close to the others, often flank to flank, the ancient solace of touch.

She doesn't come to the fence anymore. Though she can't hear me, I still talk to her about the ebbing tide in my body, the broken bellows of breath, the flight of the hours, my loving attachment to the broken things of this world, the deep ditch between us. Some days, I sing to her.

> *Put your arms around me*
> *like a circle round the sun.*
> *Don't you do me mama*
> *like that easy rider done.*
> *Stealin'. Stealin'.*
> *Pretty mama, don't you tell on me.*
> *I'm stealin' back to my same old used to be.*

A gone comet, a seventeen-year-old cat named Shitty and the beautiful crone Shalimar roaming around in my head.

Some days there is no room for anything or anybody else. I believe the three know one another. Sometimes they touch. Their knowing holds together the world I share with them. I go as far as I can with talk. Then I weep for the words I cannot speak.

Jawbone Barks at the Annual Weekend Poetry Festival

Kent, Ohio, 2004

Jawbone is back in Kent town on Water Street where he was whelped, born one spring night in the mud, the blood and the beck, under a half moon. The other half of the moon never came back but Jawbone does each spring. He wanders into Kent to snoop around the poets to hear if they've learned anything worth knowing since last year. He listens with his big pricked ears to every word whether it be from the abundance of a poet's heart or a fleck of ash in a darkened eye.

Jawbone's favorite word is pie, sweet potato pie, hair pie, poem pie. He eats the whole pie, face first, licks the pan till it shines like a pewter dollar in a mud hole. Jawbone believes in finishing what he started. You invite him in for a cup of coffee, you better plan on him staying for more than one supper. He is no fool but he fools around. He knows that the nighttime is the right time and that the heart is never given out of the bosom in vain. Jawbone does not stand in judgment of his brothers and sisters. He does insist that poets tell the truth, the whole truth, and nothing but the truth but he loves the truth told sideways, slanted, ass backwards or preferably inside out.

All winter, in his hibernation, Jawbone been dreaming bewilderment. Oh, the freedom, the green relish, of being bewildered, not to have to know why or how, but just walk in to town buck naked wearing only the tall shining top hat of bewilderment. Bewilder means to lose someone in a pathless place, to confound for want of a plain road. The wilderness is where bewilderment wants to leave you.

The wilderness where moonlight is the only torch, where cricket children sing psalms in the shadows and the earth moves under each step, where your money is no good, nothing adds up and the great Greenland bear breaks a yellowed tooth on your stone heart and a fountain breaks forth from the hollow of your bloodied chest and you weep because this is what you have always wanted. You can't go home because it is not there anymore.

Jawbone lives in Bewilderment, Ohio, just north of Mind Heart Mountain. The trail ends in the foothills, no mailbox, just a bleached jawbone wedged between two stones. His first midnight in town each spring, Jawbone slips down to the Cuyahoga River beneath the Main Street Bridge. The Cuyahoga is running free since the city knocked out the damned dam, sending that pea soup sludge backed up pond whooshing down river, breaking like a boil on Beelzebub's butt. The skies over Kent cleared with a big Hosanna. The iron lid was lifted.

More air to breathe, more light to eat in Kent now. Jawbone wades into the Cuyahoga scrotum deep with a fresh bar of Irish Spring soap and lathers winter away, scuds of suds, domes of foam, browned and gritty, oiled and soiled, roll down river, old moldy horniness, the bad breath of unspoken prayers, curdled hopes, the old headcheese whiff of gone love, the mildew of the same scraggly fur coat all his life. Jawbone scrubs hard till the soap is gone and the Kent early May sun is climbing up over the trees. Then he slips downtown for some breakfast pie and a little hanky panky.

He is here tonight, though he'll be hard to pick out in the crowd. He loves to hide—and he can dress up like someone you almost know, that third cousin from Saskatoon, or that loudmouthed preacher you went snorkeling with in an Indiana quarry twenty years ago or the tall stranger who grasped the brass handle of your father's casket and lifted.

Jawbone moves light footed through time and does not leave tracks. Look around. You won't find him. He'll find you. Jawbone got Hollyhock pups all over town, one on every block, born to Magnolia mothers and Black Eyed Susans. They are all named Freedom, first name and last. Can't tell 'em apart. It doesn't matter. Who told you it did? Hello,

Freedom. Good morning, Freedom. I love you, Freedom. Don't you love Freedom, Freedom? Your Mama did.

Let us send up a weekend of poems to Spring, bright carnival music, bebop of the mother tongue, tiny shot glass of the haiku, stories braided like a hank of coarse black hair, the whetted edge of a single line, the hand on the drum skin, a love song for the busted hearts and the one legged dancers, for the ragweed angels and those for who the curfew has come.

Jawbone remembers and misses a gone brother, a singer of indomitable song, Daniel Thompson who wrote these words. Let's send them up.

> *Nowhere*
> *to go, let's go there.*
> *Nothing to do, let's do it again.*

Welcome to the Annual Jawbone Open Poetry Readings. Let's do it again.

Celebration of the New Mural by Cherokee Artist Edwin George

237 North Water Street, Kent, Ohio
October 16, 2005

North Water street in Kent celebrates
its own mandala, big spirit signboard
covering the whole side of a building,
God's rectangular eye watching over us.

It is a totem unfurled like a banner,
a giant snow flake emblazoned
with emblems from the world we share,
bear, bird, deer, ant, butterfly, wolf.
At the center, two turtles lean,
shell to shell, watching the sun's
red eye climb up over the Cuyahoga River.
May we be held as they hold one another.

The painting is a map.
We are all travelers on its trails.
This mural has risen like a full moon
to light our way on that journey.
No billboard this, no commercial,
but spirit work, the inward world
translated by Edwin George and those
who shaped this bright tattoo onto brick,
not with grains of colored sand,
but with paint and brush and hours.

This mural is a story, a refuge, a sweat lodge,
a sanctuary, a house for the mind to enter.
Call it a door. Step through it.
What will you find? What will find you?

Come stand here alone
at midnight, at sunrise.
Listen between heartbeats.
Hear the faint sheng of the dancers' bells behind you.

Standing Rock is just up the Cuyahoga River from here,
a council rock where warring factions met to seek the peace.
They stacked their weapons on the banks
and waded out to the rock where they found safe ground.

In that spirit, let this be declared a place of council,
safe ground, where the peacemakers are welcome.
Welcome the love makers here also
for there is no peace without love.

We have set up camp here
at North Water Street Gallery:
this community of art, music, poetry.
Inside this hoop, we cook word chowder
for the wanderers, for those who refuse
the scraps from the king's buffet.
Edwin has painted what hides from the eye.
Drums speak. Kokopelli's flute's song leads us on.

This mural is the new neighborhood flag.
A bright wallflower on a gray October day.

It is the painted face of the world.
It marks a trail to the shining path.

Clouds Pile Up in the North

These August afternoons I spend
on the front porch of the lake cottage
with the neighborhood children,
a gaggle of tadpoles cavorting
in the sparkling waters of summer.
I set up a repair shop for fishing reels,
roller skates, fire trucks and cut
bubble gum out of hair. Tend splinters.
Make dill pickle faces and wiggle my ears.

I tell them stories, how Jesus once rode
a walrus down the middle of the lake.
I saw it one midnight under the Aurora Borealis,
spiked lightning racing from pole to pole.
Where'd the walrus come from? frowns little
thumb sucking Clint. *From the manger*
right next to where Jesus was born.
Clint rolls his eyes and asks, *You got
any more red popsicles?*

Little Sarah holds up a twenty-dollar bill,
her monthly allowance, and asks, *Whose picture is this?*
That is Thomas Jefferson, the grand architect of this country.
Says here right under the picture his name is Andrew Jackson.
Yep, Old Hickory, a tough guy. Sarah rolls her eyes,
puts the twenty back into her pink sequined purse
and snaps the clasp.

Clint's toad stool-tall ninja brother Kent
wanders over to see where Clint got the
popsicle. *In the freezer. Be sure to shut the door.*

The Baptist neighbor brothers find their way
to the meeting. Beanpole Ike the Spike
and his morose little sidekick, Jake the Snake,
the tag he wears. They stand off to the side,

wearing the heavy boots of their parents' fears
in a fallen world.
You guys want a popsicle?
No, thank you.
The fisher boys, Bustin' Justin and red headed Birdman,
trudge up the sidewalk from the pier. I know
the answer, but I want to hear it from them,
their sweet, piping lilt. *You do any good?*
Nothin' but a couple of mud turtles. They got
our hooks.

Jessica, the dark shy cricket who drags
her left foot in the gravel, plays alone
as always, building a tiny castle of
sticks and stones.

I tell the children not to kill the ants
on the front porch, because these tiny creatures
are all God's children, like us,
and they are my friends.
I know their names, every ant on the hill.
The worker ants are scurrying
home to play with their kids.

Clint brings one to me
and asks, *Who's this?*
Ah, this is my good friend Brave Benny.
Clint drops Benny to the concrete
and grinds him with his size-four
Batman tennis shoe.

I tell him, *One day your heart*
Of compassion will open.
Everything will change.
Clint: *You're a fat ass.*

Summer is old.
The lake has turned over,
a murky, pungent green.
Clarity is nothing I want
anymore.

Let our closeness be such,
when you weep
I taste salt.

A Finger at the Temples

Lee Peterson Reads Her Poem in the Kiva Auditorium
Kent State University

The poet leaned at the lectern,
waiting for the audience to settle.
I sat in the tiered seats,
looking down at the stage.
Below me a young woman took
a chair in front of a hearing-
impaired student.
As the poet spoke her first words,
the signer began knitting the air
with her hands, warp and woof,
a moving tapestry for anyone
who can read that alphabet.
The tracks of birds across the winter sky
of the room, wren fingers, grackle thumb.
The quick jot, finger painting with words.
She mouthed the words to the student,
to me, busy mime. As the poet
lifted lines from the page,
I began to listen with my eyes.

>   *Stars*—quick glance up.

>   *Daffodil*—invisible flower cup
>   in the air.

>   *Mine*—flat hand to the chest.

>   *Hobbled*—needs the shoulders,
>   bound and worked back and forth.

>   *Died*—one hand on top of the other,
>   laying the body into the grave.

>   *Love making*—one fist on top
>   the other, turning.

Gone—brushing away with the hand.

Birds fly through—sweep of fingers.

End—slice with the hand.

Hunger—thumb and fingers
move down the center of the chest.

Thirst—finger traces the throat, down.

Pocket—hand plunges to the pocket.

Snipers—fingers pointed down, the
other hand chopping beneath them.

Burning Air—hands churning.

Fish—hand with erect thumb swimming
across the chest.

Know—finger at the temple.

House—lean-to of hands.

Teach me—both hands quacking at the forehead,
pulling in the world.

Rain—fingers down, like the tines of a rake.

Ground—open palms down.

Bread line—draw a line in the air, toward the mouth.

Imagination—finger twirled at the temple.

China—this sign I don't get.

Hold Me—crossed fists on the chest.

Buddha—hand drawn across the belly.

Strong—both fists pumped.

Back—thumb pointed over the shoulder.

Uphill—fingers stair stepped.

Spirit—bring the right hand down
toward the open left hand with the
palms facing, create the letter *F*,
thumb to first finger as the right hand is drawn upward,
as if unspooling a film negative, the spirit pale shadow
against blackness, spirit rising through the smoke hole
of a Hopi lodge, out of the Kiva's holy ground.

The poet comes to this:
God fills us as a woman fills a pitcher.

The sign for *God* is the flat right
hand with the palm facing left.
Move the hand in a backward-downward
arc toward self, pointing upward,
denoting God is above all.

The sign for *hand* is to place
the downturned right palm over
the back of the downturned left hand.
Move the right hand toward the self
and repeat this action with the left
hand over the right.

The pitcher wants a hand, not words.

The pitcher cannot fill or empty itself.

A Letter Finds Merle Mollenkopf on His 70th Birthday

Dear Merle,

It has been fifty years. I wonder if you even remember me. I have never forgotten you and that snowy night when you missed your bus and came into that little coffee shop where I worked till midnight. To this day, I have never met a man who could drink so much coffee. The bottomless cup, announced the sign on the window. As I leaned over the pie counter, I heard you softly remark, *The cup may be bottomless, but the waitress certainly isn't.* I turned around ready to give you a slice of homemade hell, but you raised your cup, winked, smiled and added, *A thing of beauty is a joy forever.*

You always knew what to say. I've never forgotten that smile or how you folded your arms across your chest to listen to my dreams after I closed up the shop, my hopes to get out of that gritty town, on to a place where I could spread my wings and touch nothing but sky. We talked till daybreak found us. I wanted to become a prima ballerina (I loved to say it over and over, *prima ballerina*) on a swan lake, held safe in a prince's arms, curtain calls on a stage strewn with roses.

I did finally get on stage. I send along a photograph, taken about ten years after we met that night. I was somewhere in New Jersey, I think, billed as Little Sheba, Queen of the Nile, headlining the burlesque marquee. The peacock in the photo is the real thing. When we were on stage together, I had to watch my step. Beware of the mystical eyes in his plumage. Men have gotten lost there. He can see right into a heart, the way you did that night, those few hours, all we had, that one long goodbye.

You told me about a poet you loved: Robert Frost. You had memorized one of his poems and recited it for me. I wrote down a couple of lines on a napkin and keep them, still.

Earth's the right place for love: I don't know where it's
likely to go better.

I don't remember the name of the poem, only that the trees bent over like women drying their long hair. Did you keep up with it? Memorizing Mister Frost's poems?

Do you still believe that, Merle, about earth being the right place for love? I am not so sure anymore. I do trust that my words and photo will somehow find you. You must be nearly seventy by now. Me, I haven't changed at all. I am still that young woman you remember, hair tied up in red ribbons, pouring that bottomless cup. I remain the beautiful Sheba, the reigning queen of the Nile, a joy forever.

Conversation with William E. Towers

The remnants of last week's hurricane
crawl into northeast Ohio,
a gray dance of drizzle.
I call handyman Billy Towers, floating around
in his bathtub of warm beer, a third-
floor one-room home overlooking the parking lot
of the Veterans of Foreign Wars.

Sorry, no work here today, Billy. Too wet to
paint in my basement. Too wet to plow.

God Bless you, brother, says Billy. *I just woke up.*
Every man is innocent in his dreams.
May you be caught in the rapture of
the things of this world and not by those
in the next. And don't you drink too much of that wobble pop.

How's your daughter Megan? Billy asks.

She's working at home health care, driving
around Portage county in her old Toyota
helping Medicaid folks, God's wounded children.

Billy says, *That's hard work. You gotta*
weep with the ones that weep. But,
you tell her don't go walking in Bitter
Creek. If she hears her voice
getting crackly and grouchy, it's time
to get out.

And, Maj, you take that little man who's
dancing on your chest and put him
back inside. Oh, you got a jewel
in your heart. And tell everybody
you meet today to have mercy before
judgment. God bless you, brother.

God bless you, Billy, this gun-metal gray day.

For My Daughter Meg, Graduating from Kent Roosevelt High School

Monarch butterflies find their way
through days and nights and storms, across the gulf
to winter, sleeping in the dark trees of Mexico.
No map. They know where home is.
Look for your teachers.
They have come a long way to meet you.
An old woman who talks to the wind.
A child who weeps and draws pictures in the dirt.
A beautiful young man, his face painted
in colors you've never seen.
The teacher may not be a person,
but a storm that carries away your house,
a blossoming dogwood that walks about
while you sleep.

Love and death are wondrous gifts.
Few open them.
Don't fail to open the gifts.
Your actions are your only
true belongings.
Nothing else is yours.

Be a love dog. Howl for what you love.
Refuse the chain, the fence,
the little house that keeps you
from the rain.

You are a quick river in a green time,
finding your way to a great sea
that will call to you all your life.
Never forget you begin somewhere
in the mountains, far to the north
where snow and sky join.

Business of the Day

Today, I plunked down two hundred and eighty-two dollars
on a bright-white, sparkle-clean dishwashing machine
and hooked it to the buried river of Mama's tears
that cuts its way under this town.
My wife and I loaded it with every crusted plate,
egg yolk fork and dirty thought we could find.
I twisted one of its black eyes, and it lurched to life,
this creature named Caloric, fathered by Amana.
The heat, as it slushes dirt to shining death,
is measured in British Thermal Units,
who fear nothing except
popsicles and cold kisses.
Wash, dirty, wash, dirty, wash.

Back where we started,
where it will end one day.
Picture all of this sitting on
the head of a cobra coiled
on the back of an elephant which stands
upon a turtle, with another turtle beneath,
turtles all the way down.
Then more nothing.

II

This evening, in the Acme supermarket,
I locked carts with Patrick O'Flaherty,
the Kent poet who breaks language over his knee
and taunts the gods with his didgeridoo.
I asked him, in the cereal aisle,
with its menagerie of sugar-frosted creatures,
Those movies, the ones that keep
your winter soul awake. Give me a name.
Spirit of the Beehive, said Patrick.

It changed my life. You watch it once,
say goodbye to your old ways of
seeing the world.

III

At the register, I have already begun to say my farewells
to the bar code buzz, to the black conveyor belt grab.
The young cashier, the beekeeper's daughter, asks,
Plastic or paper bags? I have no answer.
Her eyes tell me her love was stolen long ago
by a man in a moon, his pale, cool kiss.
Even now she is dreaming of a small red tent,
a field of lavender, at the edge of the cold sea.

Doctor Williams' Plum Tree

for Angela

William Carlos Williams' small poem
To a Poor Old Woman finds her
on the city street, munching a plum,
its juices eyebrow to chin.
She finds plentitude and solace
in her ripe plums. And they taste good to her.
The professors teach this poem
as Williams' song to the quotidian blessed
by its very commonness, to the dignity
of the old ones or his splitting of the rock
and setting free an old woman as flower,
the radiant gist in her every bite.

In poetry class this morning
a lovely young woman from Greece,
who reads American secondhand,
raised a wrist of shimmering bracelets
to say, without apology,
for her the poem has only to do
with an act of love and the leaning thereto.
You can see it by the way
the old woman gives herself to the one
half of the plum sucked out in her hand.
This is what it means, she said.

How it must warm Williams' bones,
buried in a book, to be received this way,
by such a plum tree of a woman,
blossom all about her,
and bending to his poem.

East Liverpool Mantra

January, a break in the weather.
I drive two hours south down
to Mountaineer Park, West Virginia,
to play the cheap claimers.

At the Traveler's Hotel in downtown East Liverpool,
just across the Ohio river from the track,
the weekly rate hotel neon marquee spells *ROOMS* in three-
foot letters.
Three of the letters are burned out—*R O* and the *S*.
Only *OM* lights up, flashing *OM*,
dark, then *OM*, dark, *OM*.
Lots of empty rooms in East Liverpool, Ohio.
No continental breakfast,
but a jewel in every lotus.

A retired Ford factory guy
at the Mountaineer Park rail
grouses that years ago he played golf
rather than horses, but his legs got old,
the holes got smaller
and the balls got bigger.

Old daddy duffer, me and
five hundred and seventy-eight other pilgrims
push through the turnstiles
to pay our respects this gray day.

Keeping the Word: The Horseplayer's Creed

I tell John, my track rat partner,
if the four horse doesn't win this race,
I'll eat that guy's hat, pointing
to a big old boy in a red baseball cap
with a gold Marlin logo. Looks brand new.

My horse *Secondhandrose* struggles home fifth.
John leans over to big Bob and asks
if he'd hand over the hat so I can make
lunch out of it. I'm thinking, where
do I start? Maybe the brim.
The plastic strap on the back
will be the hardest to get down.

Naw, says Bob, *he don't want to eat my hat.*
And I don't. Bob knows as well as I do
that men too often say things we don't mean
and that not everything counts.
Besides, Bob likes that hat.

He also liked the two horse,
a plodder named *Noname Storm*
who finished a washed-out sixth,
walking home behind my *Secondhandrose.*

Twelve minutes till the next race.

Poverty, That Flower

June 1, 1995, River Downs,
Cincinnati, the fourth race,
for $7500 claimers.
The winner at odds of 26 to 1
was a horse named *Poverty*.
He paid $53.60 to win.
I didn't have him.
Another winner I let get away.

I'll be go to hell
if I'll put my money
on a horse named *Poverty*.
And I won't love a woman
named Oblivion,
won't name my kids
Sin and Evil.

Some things I just won't do.

Living in the Margin

I telephone my off-track betting service,
1-800-DOLLARS to place
my first bet of the day, at Philadelphia Park,
a speedball named *Another Alphabet.*
Lone speed is always dangerous.

I hear a recorded message welcoming me,
assuring me they appreciate
my business, that I should punch up #1
on my touch tone, to speak to a live operator.
I get Diane, honeyed, smoky, silky voice.
She wants my account number and my secret
password—I can tell her, not you.
You have $243.03 in your account.
Where we goin', honey?

The knucklehead who lives in me
thinks of all kinds of stupid answers
to her question: *Where we goin', honey?*
For all I know, Diane may be asking
the question I have been waiting on for years.

But, I tell her, *Philadelphia, upcoming race,*
$10 to win on the #2 horse.

So much we never dare
to say to one another.

These Blues

He was sitting on the sidewalk slumped against the front wall of the Kent CVS. Late sixties, cutoff jeans, ragged tie-dye tee shirt, broken down, unlaced boots, white beard, fighting the heat with a tall Arizona iced tea nesting in a clump of plastic bags. Sun and wind tanned, off the road, off the river, off the map. My wife Lu and I pulled into a parking space near him. She ran in while I waited in the car. I saw him ask something of a college student passing by. The young man mouthed a casual *no* and quickened his step.

When Lu came back, I handed her a creased five dollar bill. She offered it to him. A mumbled *thanks. Someone stole his belongings*, she said. He sat, head down, reading the concrete. I gave her twenty bucks. When he took it from her fingers, he stared at it and began to weep. Twenty five dollars would not change his lot nor bring back what had been lost. I offered him my open palm. He held up his palm, that ancient gesture, no weapon, no fear, a friend. He then struggled to his feet, leaning on a handmade wooden cane and walked to the car. He seemed intent on bringing me a message, something more than thanks. What he said, at the open car window, sounded like, to my garbled hearing, *These Blues, 13, 1 & 2.*

I am a man who spends his waking hours scouring for signs, starlight chatter, mosaics of broken conversations, every outward sign pointing inward, a volunteer transcendentalist. My morning prayer is *may the messenger come, this day.* And I am a hard-scrabble gambler, a horse player, addicted beyond recall, bedeviled by bad luck, wrong choices and busted trifectas. When he spoke, I heard what the believing heart always hungers for, the voice crying out of the present wilderness, prescience, redemption, offering what I took to be the name of a winning horse, *These Blues*, along with the exacta 1/2 in the 13th race.

Believe with me here. This didn't look like the messenger I expected. CVS is not an off-track betting parlor. But, this had to be the guy, finally. My curses had been answered. *What? These Blues?* I asked. I wanted to get it right. If I had the name of the horse and the race, I could find the track anywhere in America and make the bet on the phone. *No, No,* he said, scowling, *Hebrews: 13, 1 & 2.* This time I got it. From the Bible. Chapter and verse. It never was about horses.

Back home, I opened mom's old Bible to *Hebrews: Chapter 13, 1 & 2.*

> *Be not forgetful to entertain strangers: for thereby some have entertained angels unawares. Remember them that are in bonds, as bound with them; and them which suffer adversity, as being yourselves also in the body.*

To have entertained angels unawares. Over the years, I have been conned, hustled, bamboozled, robbed, stole from, duped, worked, bilked, shook down, slicked and tripped up. This didn't feel like that; it is through our feelings that we come to know the world. The old stories tell us of how the gods and the emissaries disguise themselves to test our faith, our imagination, to remove the bandages from our eyes. CVS . . . Celestial Visitation Summertime. CVS . . . Christ's Vagrant Son . . . wandering across the Milky Way. The Chinese have named it the River of Heaven. Angels drift through here. Not those androgynous, winged, robed, hovering attendants, but more like us. Some get tired of swimming against the current in this muddy river.

> *Be not forgetful to entertain strangers: for thereby some have entertained angels unawares. Remember them that are in bonds, as bound with them.*

So I am bound to him, bound as he is bound. This time I am the guy in the car, with the money. This could all change in a heartbeat. Will change.

The Sufis call this old angel, this cloud man who sits on concrete, *Khidir*, a teacher, a presence, an enduring spirit, who travels through time, embodying himself in whatever form is appropriate for the lesson at hand.

Look hard at the world for what it has to teach us. Remember that there are other worlds inside this one.

When a pickpocket looks at a holy man, all he sees is his pockets.

As I backed out of the lot and took a last look, I told Lu, *I wish I'd given him everything I have.*

That was last Sunday. Every day I have looked for him. No sign. Whatever I've learned, whatever happened between us, will have to be enough. *Hebrews: Chapter 13, verses 1 & 2.*

II

You cannot wrap fire in paper

Farm Market

Yesterday, at the deli, Krieger's market,
as an old man was handed his paper-wrapped
meat cuts over the counter, he thanked
the young woman, the butcher's beautiful daughter,
with *God Bless You*. As I rolled my cart by him,
I offered, *And God Bless You*. He replied,
God Bless You, smiling with his eyes.

This is God's grateful man, trailed down the aisle
by the great angel Gabriel, dragging the tips
of his heavy wings across the cold concrete floor,
Gabriel, juggling a galaxy of potatoes, pears,
oranges, avocados, apples, Gabriel, whistling
rainbow, carnival, covenant.

Bless you wherever you find yourself this day.

The Men in the Mountain

We pull into the Walgreen's parking lot, corner of 10th Ave. North and 22nd St., Saint Petersburg Beach, Florida. My daughter Meg runs in to pick up her photographs, 24 hour quick service, free double prints. I wait in the car. A green Taurus station wagon noses into the next space, disgruntled woman at the wheel, stare-straight-ahead space kids strapped into the back seat.

At the convenient mart across the street, the doors open, close, open, brake lights, back up lights, sliding out into the traffic, cars reclaiming their spots. In the middle of buzz-rush 22nd St., right in front of me, a car stalls, a white Plymouth Reliant. A young woman grinds at the starter. Emergency blinkers. The bulky woman, in a palm tree tee shirt, jumps out to raise the hood. The dead engine won't answer. Two young firemen, in blue tee shirts and shorts, stroll, from the station across the street, through the traffic, to offer their help. She refuses, gets back in to crank the starter. The men, rebuffed, dawdle, leaning on the fender. Reliant chortles to life in a fart of a blue-white smoke. Miss CanDo slams down the hood, jumps in and bolts away.

The idle firemen return to their folding chairs in front of the station; behind the doors are parked the trucks, gassed and wide eyed. It is dusk. The cars slip along in their silence. No one looks at anyone else. All the windows are closed for the Florida summer.

My folks bought me a record when I was ten years old, a big vinyl disk, hubcap size, the new technology of 1950 conjuring a bodiless voice in my room. I could start and stop it or drag my thumb on the spinning record and make the voice slow down. It was mine, the world inside the record and the little red plastic player. The voice sounded as if it belonged to a school principal or a police chief, someone in charge who knew how to entertain and instruct children.

The narrator told me the story of an Indian who was hunting, wandering in the mountains when night fell. He was far from his camp. He found a cave, went to sleep and, for some reason I never understood, slept, like Rip Van Winkle, for a hundred years.

When he woke, he stumbled out into a world he no longer knew. Where there had been camps of teepees, he saw cities (though he didn't know the word) with buildings (my word, not his) scraping Father Sky. Where there had been dirt trails, concrete roads ran in all directions. And here was the strangest part: all the people were riding inside little houses on wheels, looking out the windows but not at one another. Always moving. When the Indian tried to walk on the hard trails, the little houses honked like angry geese and the people behind the windows shouted at him, shook their fists.

Gone was the grass, the game he hunted. Gone were his people. It was no longer a world he could live in. At sunset he went back to the cave and never came out again. I listened to the story over and over. I couldn't figure out why he went back to the cave, that dark, dank world, why he didn't get his own little house on wheels in his favorite color and start moving.

Fifty years later, in the warm February dusk, I am sitting in a Walgreen's parking lot, watching the scuttling little houses begin to turn on their porch lights. One honks like that angry goose at another who has crossed the yellow boundary line. I look out the windows of my little house on wheels; all around me, bright signs hang words up to the eye. *Clearance. Sale. No Money Down. Buy Now. Pay Later. Stop.*

Everywhere the thick dead skin of asphalt. Ugliest word in the language. Ass fault. Your ass, my ass, somebody's ass, is at fault. Gaia, our green mother, entombed under the ass fault. The concrete, the asphalt, the blank faces, the churn of ozone and breath, the gray fields, the dead zones.

How will we live without it? That beauty without which the soul is starved into rancor, then silence. I slump in the seat, trying to defend myself with memories of natural beauty, a shield held up against this place. The booming stillness of the gray Tetons across Lake Jackson, the double image in the living waters. A woman standing bare breasted, hands on hips, at a window in the morning light, her nipples crowned mouths that whispered my secret name. The Embarras River, the open vein of my childhood in Illinois, its flood tide current cutting through the spring green of woods, tugging at red bud limbs in half blossom. The Great Triangle of Summer rising in the East above the farm fields. The last light of the day kissing the tops of the Cypress grove near the home place, bones of trees, bones of my fingers, tracks in fresh snow.

The back car door opens. Meg is back with the photos, hands me the change, a dollar and coins. Our little Oldsmobile house on wheels pulls out into the asphalt current, painted arrows pointing us home.

There are no mountains in Florida, no caves, other than those sinkholes of blue, bottomless water. The caves, like the kingdom of heaven, are within. If you should die before you wake, I pray the Lord your soul to take.

Find the Poem in the World

At the corner where North Lincoln Street dead ends at Crain Avenue in Kent, in a bare tree over the roadway, hangs a hornet's nest, a globe of paper-thin patchwork, a sky dome constructed with chewed wood fiber mixed with saliva, an abandoned piñata.

Inside the nest's hard shell are three to four tiers of combs: bunk beds and pantry. A small opening at the bottom is the portal between that world and this. A colony of hornets—or social wasps—lives only one year. Their season is quartered as is ours: egg, larva, pupa and adult. The adults abandon the nest in the fall after the first hard freeze. The queens are the only members of the colony to survive the winter. Each nest is built anew in the swell of spring.

In April or May, each queen hunts for a new home, builds a small nest and begins the task of raising sterile daughter offspring. These take over the work of constructing the nest, foraging for food, caring for the young. The queen lives only to produce more eggs. Broods emerge and the work goes on. With the approach of fall, males and new queens emerge. These leave the nest and mate. The fertilized queen hibernates, a small death from which she will awaken. The rest of the workers, the deposed queen and the males die of old age or cold.

The old queen is asleep in her milkweed chamber. She and her lovers are dreaming of a spring that will never come.

None of us sees the same world, though we live in it. In the trees over Crain avenue, a dead star, a bandaged, blind eye, the ruins of an abandoned city, a priest's hollow heart, the lost head of the Halloween horseman, the drinking gourd of thirsty Jesus, a gray squid washed ashore in a treetop, the muddied mind empty of words.

When we make the poem, wood pulp paper, black spittle ink,
we build a refuge for ourselves and others, a shelter house.
Poetry is the house that poems built, line by line, spit, tears
and word. It will not save us. Time and cold claim all, even
the queen, that sorrowful mother. It is respite, a temporary
shelter where we may learn and listen to one another's hearts.

Go there. Look up. Know this:

We live inside more worlds than we can count.

What we call sky is our own making.

To love is to serve.

To work is to love.

Some leave. Others remain.

The frost is the cold breath
of a god who forgives us everything.

There is a single door: egress, enter.

Beyond that is a nameless silence.

We will not be together here again.
The hornet's nest is finished,
as best we could.
It is time to leave before the deep cold.

Let us raise high what we have done here,
hoist it into the open arms of the World.

For Marv Smith/A Farewell

February 5, 1932 – September 14, 2006

The calendar, that open book counting our days,
marks tonight, October 7, 2006, as the full Hunter's Moon.
The skies over northeast Ohio are as clear as spring water.
The moon will boom up out of the dark trees.
Something blind and loving in me, in each of us,
will rise to meet it, the nameless man in the moon
who watches as we sing and we sob and we plant and we reap.
The cold stone eye in the heavens.
The full Hunter's Moon with an empty belly.
We hunt. We are hunted. We seek shelter in one another.

In small print in the calendar square naming this day
are these words from Hawthorne: *Moonlight is sculpture.*
The living cannot understand this, any more than
we can hear moonlight's frozen music.
Marv Smith has slipped through the curtain.
He no longer works in words, glass, metal, ink, clay.
He is now a sculptor of moonlight,
shaping that pale fire with his hands
that cannot forget what they have learned.

Raise high the moonbeam, Marv.
Though you must make your new home in shadow,
in the dry sea of the Sorrowful Mother's tears,
finish the work you began here.

Sculpt the moon's hard light.
Glaze it with fine, gray ash.

Gathered Under the Full Wolf Moon

It had been a couple of years since I'd heard from Wild Bill Towers, who once wandered the streets of Kent speaking beatitudes to the trees, now camped out in the mesquite around Mesilla, New Mexico. He used to call me an old lion and reminded me that every heart is a jewel. Last night, Bill called to tell me he has just bought a teepee and LuAnn and I are welcome to come stay as long as we want. He read me a new poem he'd written, the kind that never ever turns up in poetry writing workshops, a poem I could live on for a week. I copied it down.

> *A young coal miner,*
> *crawling on his belly*
> *with a short, small pick,*
> *had great big balls and a great big dick.*
> *He could see in the dark.*
> *He'd rather cut his wrists*
> *than go underground.*
> *He couldn't cuss.*
> *God wouldn't let him*
> *because he had a baby son around.*

This is a poem for me. It is all heart, all love, raw, no packaging, no smirk in behind the knowing. Not artful presentation. This poem knows what is precious. Tenderness before mercy. Then mercy before judgment.

The midpoint of winter. All downhill toward spring from here. I have been spending too much money and time these gray, snowy afternoons playing horses simulcast from around the country. The infernal satellite dish, that concave blind eye, is bolted to the roof of our house. It feeds the horse races right into my living room. From palm tree lined Gulfstream in Miami, from sun-kissed Santa Anita in Los Angeles. I am right there as long as I don't look out the window here in Kent into the whiteout. I got a telephone betting account—$58.41 to the good as of this moment. It is a hard way to make a living. A strange, capricious god presides over this business. Accept loss forever and get on with it.

Most days I feel as dumb as a bag of rusted hammers, as boneheaded as Oedipus searching for himself. Yet I play on, putting my shoulder to Ezekiel's wheel, that shining celestial hubcap. My one winner last night was at Delta Downs. I was in balmy Louisiana, at least during the 8th race. I doubled all my money, short odds. The horse's name was *All Time*, a front runner. Early speed holds up at Delta. It is the action I love, contending with the faceless god Chance, the god with two left hands, one open, the other closed. It is squarely between me and him.

I have been trying to get ready for the winter by reading Anton Chekhov's short stories again, their beautiful tenderness, their puzzlement over what it means to be human. I bought a portable collection of Chekhov stories at *Last Exit Books* here in Kent—for $2.50, used. What does it mean that a book is "used" and worth less than a new one? Are some of the words lost or worn out? Lebron James signs a contract with Nike for ninety million dollars—and I can buy the sweet fruit of Chekhov's genius for $2.50. How do we assign such value to things? What brand of shoes has that young coal miner got laced on? The dark doesn't care.

The poet, my friend Mac Lojowsky, once phoned me from Moscow, his drunken heart lifting off from California and dragging him across half the world. I asked him to search for Anton Chekhov's grave, to thank him for me. He found it amidst the pomp of the military and politicians, marble stallions reared, the dead mouths of cannons. Chekhov's grave is marked by a simple stone in a galaxy of monuments: *Anton Pavlovich Chekhov, January 17, 1860 – July 2, 1904.* Mac spoke our names over his grave and said he 'bout froze his ass off doing it. Later, Mac got caught trying to piss on Lenin's tomb. The police roughed him up before turning him free. Mac is used to that kind of thing.

I copied Chekhov's words in my notebook:

> *My holy of holies is the human*
> *body, health, intelligence, talent,*
> *inspiration, love and absolute*
> *freedom—freedom from violence*
> *and falsehood, no matter how*
> *the last two manifest themselves.*

And this, speaking of himself, and for all who wish to be free.

> *Write how this youth squeezes the*
> *slave out of himself drop by drop,*
> *and how, waking one fine morning,*
> *he feels that in his veins flows*
> *no longer the blood of a slave*
> *but that of a real man.*

My work this day: to squeeze the slave out of myself drop by drop and word by word. Poem by poem. You can't tell the difference by looking at me. I squeezed hard today, for a few drops. The work is long. There is not enough time. Drop by drop. In the cold. In the dark.

Fancy Gap

They call it Fancy Gap,
North Carolina, a cut
east/west through the Blue Ridge.
I am parked in the side lot
of Shoney's restaurant,
my head back, catching the morning sun,
eyes closed, a break from the
eleven hundred-mile Florida drive back to Cleveland.
I hear him sweeping behind me,
Whisk, whisk, the metal scrape of the dust pan.
He hunts cigarette butts, bottle caps,
detritus from the caravan on I-77.
A big guy, broken-down feet, jeans,
blue ball cap, working the asphalt rink,
Shoney's Zamboni man.

Good Morning.
Mornin', he grins.
I offer him my hand, my name.
He is Tommy Justice, from up West Virginia way.
Now he lives in Fancy Gap.
How come they call the town Fancy Gap, Tommy?
Ain't no town, just a gap.
Wind whips through 60-70 miles an hour, turns over
semis, cars. Nobody knows when it's coming.
Why they call it Fancy? I ask.
Don't rightly know. I just live here.

I worked in the coal mines fifteen
years in West Virginia till a 500-pound rock fell on me.
I was under what they call a kettle hole, bracing it up,
when it fell, the rock across my back.
Took six men half an hour to get it off me.
My brother was there. He pulled me out.
When I got home, I told
the wife, I'll never go in that hole again.
We moved down here to Fancy Gap.

Look, here on my back, you can still
see the scrapes. He puts down the broom
and dust pan and shows me the rakes
across the middle of his back like the
nails of an angry hand. *The worst part*
of all that was working in the dog holes.
A tunnel no bigger than for a dog to
crawl through. I brought out chunks
of coal clamped between my knees.

The talk trails off here.
Tommy Justice leans on his broom
and looks up at the cloudless sky.
My eyes follow his, up into
the empty kettle hole of heaven.

Sleepless with Mussolini

My plan was, that summer of 1955,
to steal time from death, by sleeping
only every other night.
I was fourteen. I thought
it worked that way.
We lived by a small lake in Illinois.
On the sleepless nights,
I'd be out on the water by three a.m.,
to drift and fish the false dawn.

I believed all kinds of things then.
The stars were gypsy campfires
on the lake floor; I could hear them singing.
Near the old brick tower was a cave
where a black catfish, head the size
of a car hood, ate the sins
of the fresh drowned.
In the deep beyond Boatman's Point,
a beautiful woman was weaving me
a cloak of armor, of hair and willow skin.

Though I didn't know how
to love anybody,
I wanted to be loved obsessively,
the way Billy the Kid loved killing,
the kind of love that spawned the atomic bomb
and ruined Catherine the Great.
I floated over this kingdom,
in a small wooden boat,
sustained, my bones charmed.

The night the green fireball burned
across the Midwest, I never looked up.
The water was green flame.
I was to be a man who reads water,
not sky. Now when I walk,

I do not look up.
Not that I do not want to meet your eyes,
I am busy with water, with the rivers
that run under the sidewalks.
There are stars shining beneath us.

That summer I was after an old bass,

named Mussolini by the locals.
I'd seen him once, under Maas' pier,
as long as a man's arm,
thick as a football, hidden
in the shade of a piling.
Fisherman dangled every bait:
a silver minnow, a painted night crawler,
a Luna moth, a priest's ear,
a child's promise, an abalone crucifix,
a live hummingbird, a bare hook.
Nothing worked.

I made it through July before
I broke the rosary of sleeplessness
and settled into my flesh.
I remembered what the Italians
had done to their Mussolini:
the murder of El Duce and his mistress,
stripped and strung by the heels
in the town square.
A lesson to the ruthless
that power, like love, wanes.

Old mossback Mussolini swims
into the spawning grounds one night a year
to spread his milt.
He lives deep.
He has never slept.
He hangs in shadow,
a moon in another sky.

Test the Spirits, to See Whether They Are from God

My wife Lu is forcing winter bulbs into flower,
paper-white Narcissus and red Amaryllis,
on the sill, facing the west. It is good to be
in their company, the lemony sweet fragrance
of the paper-whites, the cluster of small, inquisitive faces
leaning toward us, the red broken heart of the Amaryllis,
prying itself open like a double fist. It is not their time,
late January. Set them in warm soil, offer fake spring rain
from a faucet, pallid sunlight from a window and they bloom.
Forced into blooming.

The flower bulbs remember my wife's hands
as a cheek remembers tears.

A Nest of Stories

I

A golden hammer cracks the hard case
of the meat heart, the nut buried in the chest.

Climb the one hundred stone steps, the Inca Temple
at Oaxaca. Bring gifts of blood oranges,
black ropes of braided hair. The secret keeper,
his name is Ramon Jimenez Ojeda, is a stone
cutter from the village below. In his tenth year,
he apprenticed himself to the gods. He tells
every seeker what they did not wish to hear: the real world
is beyond the senses. Words are smoke.

On Mount Errigal, Ireland, the granite is stained
with brush strokes of blood, pale in the morning fog.

II

The Pleiades, the Seven Sisters, climb the starry ladder
into the fall sky. A purse caught and tore on the horn
of a quarter moon. The coins fell to earth in a meteor
shower of silver. The Sisters recovered all but one coin.
The number 7 is welted on each side, along with the
cipher to a forgotten language. If you find it, you must
return it, whatever the cost. If you keep it, frost
will eat the world.

When you empty yourself, you are being prepared
to be filled again, whether or not you know this.

In the late-winter yard, a single anemone, a Grecian Wind-
flower, has thrust into bloom, tiny pale-yellow petals, black
heart, balanced on a toothpick leg. Name it yearning,
that jewel.

III

If I have begged when I should have given,
I pray for forgiveness as the final fruit of Christ's love.
If I have wounded the Buddha with the dull sword
forged by my stupidity, I bow once, the blade of folded
hands against my own forehead.
A cairn of evergreen cones marks a far-north grave.
Fierce, tiny ghost dogs roam a hospital bedside table,
barking at death to stay his cold hand.
Tibetan prayer flags ride the spring wind,
offering our longings to the world.
The Diamond Gate to Never Land remains sealed
to those who look backwards.
The river of this day runs ever clear.

IV

A flashing scimitar wielded by the hanged man's son
severs the head of the gorgon who has pursued
us for so long. Together, at the cliff's edge,
we watch it drop into the sea far below us.

The world is no more
than a dream.
God is the dreamer.

When you awaken,
you will know what to do.

Words Inked on a Federal Reserve Note

We enter that order of precious blood.

We are blessed by the strong hands of the old mother
tending the garden of dead roses.
Her gifts to us are laid out
on the snail crisscrossed sidewalk.

A small pressed flower from an Alpine meadow.
A ten-penny, rusted, flood-plain nail.
A silver heart from the chained Christ.
An old Irish broom who knows its corner.
A phoebe singing in a cage of snow.

Here twice or half is whole.

A Longing to be Pure

for Christian O'Keeffe

A covered bridge of trembling dreams
spans the earth's thin mantle.
I can see it only on certain early autumn mornings
when the sun burns the fog away.

I cross that bridge and search for you again
in a world of rusted wounds and broken words.
We have become strange to one another.
The only map we share is an inked bruised calligraphy
we must read with our fingertips. Come close.
Trace the whorl of this seashell on my skin.
The four leaf clover which marks the quarters
holding all creation in its place.
On your shoulder, I touch a tattooed Shiva dancing
atop an obsidian bowl, arms entangled
in strings of sandalwood beads.

Even the hanged man demands something from us.

Both we and stones suffer ourselves into form.

Jawbone Annual Open Poetry Readings/
May 2009, Kent, Ohio

Jawbone time.
For more than twenty years now,
poets and story tellers have gathered in Kent,
in the springtime, around May Day, word fest,
crown of dandelions, lilac breath, dogwood buzz,
last rites for the snowman at the edge of the
parking lot.

We jawbone at each other with our poems.
That river rolls on. Tonight we wade in.
Let's all get wet, throw our clothes in a pile,
pick out something that doesn't fit—and wear it.

Talk your heart's talk. Love is a big bell
that rings on the hour, whether
or not you hear it. This isn't about putting
the ball in the basket or the weenie in the bun
or making sure we get what we want.

This is about how the stars watch us with
their cold, loving eyes, how the trees walk
about while we sleep, how children are older
than their parents, how shoes would dream
of walking were there no feet in the world,
how somewhere the iron tree breaks into
blossom, how we awaken empty and each
morning the day pours itself into us until we are full.

Jawbone believes there is a secret medicine
given only to those who hurt so bad they cannot hope.
That secret medicine is in poems.
You don't need a prescription.
This pharmacy is open all night long,
lights burning, bonfires on heaven's ramparts.

Jawbone is a believer in things unseen,
a tightrope walker on the wireless.
Jawbone believes there are tears inside everything,
in the moonlight, in the sidewalks, in me, in you.
Jawbone drinks from a thermos of hot tears.
He bakes his bread with burning tears.

Jawbone believes you are the voices
of this place. It will not hear itself
without your words.
Jawbone is gonna listen to every word,
bear witness, whatness, wetness,
till the last bell in the last hell.
The last leaven in the farthest heaven.

Jawbone's gonna hang around this shack
till the mail train comes back,
rolling in his sweet baby's arms.
Jawbone says everything perishes
except your heart.
Chew on that bone.

Everything perishes except your heart.
Jawbone broke apart the letters
of the heart and found they
still spell earth.

Tonight we welcome
the give it all away poets,
the give 'em heaven poets, the give 'em hell poets,
the poets who roar like lions at the gate,
the fart just loud enough to be heard poets,
the gun slinger poets, the Vaseline slide away poets,
the poets who dance in the wound,
the poets who bless us with their breath,
with their presence,
the poets who pour oil on the troubled waters,
poets who throw a match on it.

The poets who hitchhiked away from the cradle,
poets who seek shelter in the arms of others.
The patched up poets held together
by glue, string and spit.
The angel poets who work under the streets
and have never seen the sun,
the angel poets whose wings burn,
the night crawler poets out of whom
the sun rises, those poets who believe heaven
is a giant iron pot where old men and old women
soak and sing and are young again.

Jawbone wants you to tell your own truth.
Wants you to be a lamp unto yourself.
Wants you to drink from your own well,
to sing like a goldfish in a crock pot of whiskey,
to praise what hurts.

Time to walk in the dark in your new best clothes.

Gypsies in the Olive Grove

Meg, my ten-year-old daughter, and I come back to Dion, an hour's drive down the Greek coast from Thessaloniki. Dion, a tiny village in the eastern foothills of Mt. Olympos, where an earth goddess had been worshipped in prehistoric times, a goddess of fertility whose veins are open springs. Dion, as early as fifth century B.C., the *axis mundi* of northern Greece. Phillip II celebrated his victories here; his son Alexander sacrificed and prayed on this ground. We fly back to America in four days. I won't find my way here again. Meg has made plans to come back when she turns twenty. She has made a friend in Anna, the taverna keeper's daughter who is teaching her Greek.

There is a lovely, soft breeze in the cottonwoods, down along the stream where the sanctuary to Isis, a goddess whose seed must have flown the Mediterranean from Egypt, was unearthed only in 1978. She had been covered by mud and water after an earthquake in the second century A.D. Isis, her stone self, was found *in situ* on her pedestal. She is also called Isis Lochia, a patroness of women in childbirth and a patroness of good luck. I can no longer tell the difference between the voice of the breeze and that of the springs which begin in the cold heart of Mr. Olympus, go underground and surface miles below in the plain of Dion. Would that I could move without my body, hide in the earth, reappear, in the morning light.

A Greek father and son come to set their nets in the brook that skirts the sanctuary. The father throws the net from one shore to another; the boy catches it and pulls the net across. The bottom is weighted and sits taut, catching whatever comes downstream, darters, a sandal, a gold helmet, mountain trout, a Macedonian ghost who cannot pick his way clear of the mesh. The father sloughs upstream in his big rubber boots, to set more nets. The boy drags the throw line behind him, head down, a reluctant worker, trudging toward what has to be done. The third fisherman is the grandfather who stands on the bridge and directs the setting of the nets, loudly, shaking his cane that he be heeded.

From the edge of the dig, I look down on the small stone votive table where, twenty five hundred years ago, the faithful made sacrifices of animals. I remember a huge golden carp my father and I hooked one spring day in an Illinois lake. It was beautiful, high-shine black along the dorsal, gold coin scaled, wild eyed, whiskered, grunting and angry. Dad filleted him with a hacksaw. Today I lay the carp, tall as the fisherman's son, on the stone altar of Isis Lochia and open him with one deep cut from his gills to his broad tail. His blood is for the goddess of this place. I mark my cheekbones.

I lie with my eyes closed, the back of my head on the hard ground above the sanctuary, and drift with Kabir's riddle about the nature of love. *Suppose you had to cut off your own head and give it to someone: what difference would it make?* I don't know the answer. I do know the statue of Aphrodite Hypolympidia—she *who is worshipped below Olympos*—was found headless in the muddy excavation of the sanctuary. It was the villager Nicos who found her head half buried in the stream bank. He carried the head to the statue; it fit Aphrodite's neck seamlessly. The locals have come to call this Aphrodite *Nicos' Woman*. It did make a difference that the head fit. Does my head fit your body? Kabir will tell you the truth: *this is what love is like.*

Looking south down the Aegean coast, I see the nipple of Ossa, another holy mountain, a modest, girlish breast cupped to the sky. This afternoon, on the Katerina *paralia*, a young woman walked by me bare breasted, pendulous melon breasts swinging with each step. I could not speak to her. My words would have made no difference.

The gypsies are busy in their little trucks, selling plastic tables and chairs and vegetables. A truck bed crated full of tomatoes, four riders to a Datsun front seat, small faces, dark eyes. The father, over a loud speaker mounted atop the cab, barks a carnival shorthand, up and down the dirt streets of Dion.

Last month, driving west of Thebes, I came upon a valley of olive groves, mile after mile. Then, bright clothes began to appear in the dusty green trees, hung from the limbs, then red and blue blankets and shawls, then one camp and another. In a circle, in a clearing, sat a man with long white hair, a patriarchal magus, a Romanian hipster king, presiding over the circle of women and girls, his big brown hands steadied on an ornate silver cane.

At his side was the most beautiful woman I have ever seen, the color of a deep bruise, brown into yellow, with a heavy rope of black hair over her shoulder and down into her lap. I didn't see her for more than a few seconds as I drove by. She did not look up. I had nothing to offer her other than my head which I thought of tumbling into the musky basket of her purple skirts.

I made my way up out of the valley and on to the Peloponnese. It was May Day, the first day of May, when the Greeks take to the country, picking wildflowers and weaving them into garlands. The gypsies shape wreathes of bright cloth. I weave a garland of her purple skirts, her braid, the fine dark hair of the inner thigh, the silver undersides of the olive leaves. I make a hidden sanctuary for this tinker king's daughter, for both of us, in a grove sacred of the Bacchae. She moves in me like spring water, gather and drop and drop again, disappearing into the earth.

I Wish to Be Warmly Received

On the Eve of My 68th Birthday

I am threading my way through Kent's
midnight back streets after an evening
at Ciccone's bar, three Rolling Rocks
and a shot of Jim Beam, that distiller,
killer, recruiter of the woe begotten.
I don't drink much these days,
wary of consorting with spirits,
with its promises of absolution and ascension,
how it might clarify the muddied river of love,
how it stirs the ache to be known,
only to wash me ashore next morning picked clean and salt licked.

I make it home, no red and blue lights
branding me outlaw, maimer of the sober.
My wife Lu has left on the back porch light.
I sit for a long time in the car, watching
the broken movie in my head, the bar scenes:
the waitress' tattoos, the spangled jukebox,
the oyster, the pearl, the bone-headed cannibal
who ate the clown even though it tasted funny.
Inside, Lu sleeps warm, on her right side,
under a blue quilt I share.

The houses, the street, the trees,
appear fixed in the same place
as when I left hours ago,
but voices whisper I live on a funny gossamer street,
in a web with no spider, nothing here
more substantial than a cloud against a blue sky
or a breath on a frosty night.
All of it moving, ever so slowly,
melting like a glacier, into a river,
about to disappear into a black hole,
into the hunger of coal-eyed Kali,
where all worlds
begin and end.

All these years, I have been guided
only by her laughter.

Walking in the Bamboo

The first week of spring,
the Mogadore, Ohio, bait shop opens its doors.
My son and I step down into the mud
and gravel lot. We are still learning
to breathe inside the hard shell of the new year.
We both want out, though we don't say it.

Inside the concrete-block store
stands a fresh rack of willow sticks,
fly rods as tough as ligament
bonded to backbone, alive to the touch.
We hold each one at arm's length,
limbering them in the air at nothing,
tracking the long shoot of tapered line
over a deep, still pool, the dry fly
dropping light as a whisper at a midnight window.
This is the one, Sean says,
composite graphite, can't break it.

I can't tell him these days it is hard
for me to live with composite anything.
I have begun to want what is gone.
The bamboo fly rod I had when I was a kid,
no hundred dollar Heddon Black Beauty,
a cheap eight-footer, but handmade,
the hexagonal strips fitted seamlessly,
then heat welded or true tempered or wizard spitted.
It was so sure and light I could toss it
up into the summer air
and it would hang there.
I busted it on a big bass, under the shad bushes.

Up under my shirt
lives the green, crooked bamboo
that is my backbone.
I have learned to put it to use.
Each day I hoard leftovers from
the kitchen where I earn my keep.

I hide them in the hollow center
of my backbone, section by section,
rice, meat, bread, sweets.

This is how I steal food from this world
and smuggle it to the hungry ghosts in the next.
The guards never think to look there.
They nod and let me pass.

Living Room Yoga/Language of the Dog

I

My wife is practicing yoga in our living room,
a bare chested, beautiful man, Rodney Yee,
directing her every move, on the flat-screen TV.

A down dog, then, exhale.

Push up, upward dog.

Jump into a squat. Strongly flex your feet.

Open your chest.

His yoga mat is spread out in a grassy field
overlooking the blue Pacific. In the background
I see what must be Diamond Head, Hawaii.
Closer is LuAnn, following his every move.

Feel your thighbones as you touch your hamstrings.

Inhale upward dog.

I love this woman, until my last breath.
It took years for me to lift my stone heart,
the size of one of those purple exercise balls
rolling around in the tropic sunshine,
to lift it, to offer it to her.

The screen goes blank. My wife Lu rolls up her rainbow yoga mat.
She walks barefoot to the kitchen to begin the clatter of supper.

II

All day I have been staring
down into the deep throat of war,
its cold darkness, searching for the faces
of my friends the veterans with whom I work
in whose nightmares the Betties still bounce
and the Punji stick.

    Dog soldiers, dogs of war,

    upward dogs, downward dogs.

Dog tags, they are fixed to the trigger guard
on the rifle of the fallen soldier,
the rifle staked barrel down into the earth,
so he may be later identified, this downward dog.
Name, rank, serial number embossed
in the language of the living.

    Now, a downward dog, then, exhale.

    Then, open your chest.

The dead have no words for us now.
We have forgotten what they tried to tell us,
stone by stone.

Lambrini, That Flower

Tomorrow, I leave for America.
Tonight, it is goodbye
on Olgas street, Thessaloniki,
a gathering of friends
in an old Jewish villa,
everyone making mouths at one another
around the table.
The June Greek air stirs trees overhead,
awash with the heavy musk
carried from the open crotch
of Thermakos bay.

A young woman leans toward me to explain her name.
Lambrini. It means the purple flower,
blossom of resurrection, the light
that shone forth from the tomb
after the stone was rolled away.
Lambrini. The light in her face.

She tells me she lives up in the old Turkish quarter,
Ano Poulo, protected by what remains
of the ancient city walls,
where, in midsummer,
it is never wholly dark.

The Old House in Tremont, Ohio, Has Its Say

Six big glass eyes. Three big satellite ears.
Nothing gets by me in the neighborhood.
If you don't like my peeling skin,
take a hike to Pepper Pike.
I don't want to be fixed.
Do that to the cats roaming these streets.
This is who I am.

A house is a second body
for those who live within.
I guard them against every threat.
Winken, Blinken and Nod, the wee ones,
dream in their trundle beds.
Jacob, the father, who lost his job years ago,
spends his days building a boat
in my basement, out of scavenged wood.
The mother Apollonia rises before dawn
to walk the dark sidewalks to her bakery work.

I relish the laughter of the children,
the touch of bare feet on my floors,
the kiss of flame on an iron skillet,
the smells of supper, how Apollonia shines
my eyes with newspapers and vinegar,
how the Lake Erie winds make cold music
through the teeth of fencing.
They are my life.

I know that one day the boat Jacob is building
will be finished. The family will launch and sail away
across the starry seas, steering by the constellations,
guided by the lodestone in each heart.
Without them, I won't live long.
The vandals and the wrecking ball will find me.
Nothing lasts.

For now, my work is to keep the watch,
for Jacob, for Apollonia, for Winken, Blinken and Nod.
To welcome them home.

III

The hammer blows of whispered prayer,
the mapping of the unseen, that kingdom.

On the Road to Detroit

I come to hear those poets
who show us there
is more to the world
than everything in the world.

I come to hear those poets
who find ways to light the lamp
at the base of the spine,
a brief flame in the jaws of darkness.

I come here to hear those poets
with half-eaten hearts
who can forget themselves
and make their home in the Nameless.

I come to hear those poets
for whom every word is a communion wafer,
every line of a poem a strand of barbed wire,
every poem a broken Rosetta stone.

I come to hear those poets
who nail their poems to the Devil's door,
knock hard a dozen times
and do not run away.

I come to hear those poets
who hunt their own hearts out in the world,
the stone soup makers and
the thirst slakers,
those poets who are witnesses
for the defense of all
that is good in us.

Kick Starting the Poets at Last Exit Books

That beautiful, sun-washed day last week . . . Saturday . . . my wife Lu brought the wood-framed screens up out of the basement, stood them against the fence and hosed them down. After they'd dried in the sun, she threw open the windows and set in the screens, room after room. The yearly exorcism of winter, the curtains billowing out like sails of a schooner, the mean children of Jack Frost running for their lives, snow specters withering away like the wicked witch. Big deal ever since I was a kid, putting in the screens. A declaration. We go on from here, the summer, its green light.

The new Sheetz gas station opened in my neighborhood a few months ago. Its architecture is garish, a day-glow, baboon-butt red, lighted by enough megawatts to make it visible from a satellite. Goethe imagined architecture as frozen music. What kind of loony tunes is this Sheetz gas station playing? I know I should make my peace with it, go in, scarf down a couple of premixed cappuccinos and three hot dogs, fill up my tank at $3.69 a gallon, but I'm not there yet. I need to be. I have been taught that it takes courage and generosity to let the world go its own way.

The Akron Aeros minor league baseball home opener kicked off last week. I can't forget the time, about ten years ago, when a young guy dressed in a beat up trench coat on a hot summer night roamed the stadium, broadcasting the game with an old microphone with a severed cord dangling. He'd probably dug it out of a dumpster. He wandered from section to section, announcing each play. *There's a ground ball to second. The throw to first is in time. Two outs in the 5th.* Security left him alone. Nobody seemed to pay attention to him. At one point, he was a couple of rows away from me. He wore scuffed black dress shoes, no socks and, I'm guessing, no pants, with his coat buttoned from neck to knee. After a while, I began to wonder if I was the only one who saw him. It was hopeless and sad, but not to him. He smiled through it all. It was as if, to him, there would be no baseball game without his play-by-play. *There's a long one into left. It's in the gap. Two runs score for the Aeros.* Finally, he wandered off down the left field line, still calling the game.

How do we know what gets transmitted? What gets received? We have wireless transmission everywhere, more voices than people, recorded, live, the broadband abuzz. We wander through voices like an underwater swimmer through countless schools of fishes. Maybe this guy at the Aeros game was calling the Mothership. Maybe She was listening to her lost child.

We should bring an old trashed microphone and hand it around here tonight, with the conviction that a river in New Mexico slows its current to listen or that a spring willow in Sitka, Alaska, bends to hear our words or the Three Sisters of Fate pause in their work as we weave our own stories.

Pythagoras once declared, *Amazing. Everything is Intelligent.* Think hard about that when you take out the garbage or pour maple syrup on your pancakes, when you lie in the midnight grass under the Perseid meteor showers or when you give voice to your poem here tonight.

A Small Winter Meditation for the Humped

The last night of January,
I am counting out the final minutes
at Ciccone's bar, Kent, Ohio.
Bob, the owner, tells me Thistledown,
the thoroughbred track, opens
in only forty three days.
We are both counting.

A few of the jockeys have fled
south to Tampa Downs
to ride in the sunshine,
Michael Rowland, Omar Londono,
good brave little men
afraid of the cold.

I have stayed home in the freeze
to wait it out, though
snow makes me stupid,
beer makes me stupid,
and horses make me stupid.

Out in the parking lot,
the earth is tilted.
I can hardly walk it.
The darkness is deep enough to wear.

Suddenly, I remember thirty-five years ago,
a winter I spent in Saint John's
Children's Hospital, Springfield, Illinois.
A palsied, gnarled boy would stumble
laughing from room to room every morning,
pulling window blind rings down
with his teeth, making them rattle to the top,
while an old German nun chased him,
smiling and shaking her finger.
Stop that, stop that, she scolded.

It was the only work he could do.
He never missed a room,
window after window,
stunning the bedridden with light.

Strip Mining Memory

for Bob Fox, Gone Maker of Poems and Music

I was raised on a small lake, just north of Olney, Illinois. Route 130 splits Vernor Lake in two, the old city reservoir. Summers were cracked green light, moon drums, sunflower boom. Winters were harsh. The winds swept across the frozen lake, cornstalk ghosts pulling at the plastic storm windows. At the center of the cottage squatted the little cast iron gnome, the Warm Morning stove with its Isinglass eyes. It ate coal and cooked fire in its gray belly.

Dad fed it from a bucket shaped like a five-gallon gravy tureen, unhinging its jaw and pouring in the black, cracked bones dug out of the old graves of southern Illinois. This was bituminous coal, the cheap stuff at fourteen dollars a ton, strip mined by giant shovels, peeling the earth of its skin and digging down into veins. Some town folks, the Webers, the Eaglesons, the Gassmans, burned anthracite, hotter, harder, costlier, dug from tunnels closer to hell. Anthracite is sometimes called glance coal, stone coal, blind coal. All coal is blind, buried sunlight.

When Dad relit the stove those cold mornings, he built a nest of newspapers and kindling before pouring in the coal. Then, the kitchen match. The flare, the stink of sulphur. The stove restarted with a guttural *whumph* as Dad opened the butterfly damper valve on the pipe. It *took off*, Dad's words for the moment when the coal began to surrender its hidden life. Maybe this is where I started to form the notion that everyone/everything has a secret life, folded inward. For us, living in our stove bodies, suffering is the fire that calls out that life.

You cannot burn dirt. You cannot garden in a coal pile or an ash heap. You burn hidden life. Sometimes after the stove took off, Dad got lost in his first cup of coffee watching the dawn light out over the lake. He forgot to turn the damper down. The top of the stove where it joined the pipe turned cherry red, an angry phantom heartburn, an apoplectic blast off just minutes away as the fire roared up the chimney.

From my bed, piled high with quilts, I feared and longed for the whole house to go straight up like a rocket, carrying the whole family up into orbit. We would always be together. We would never die, but like that lucky old sun just roll around heaven all day. When Dad turned down the damper, throttled down the air, the stove's heart throb would slow till we couldn't hear it.

Before he left for work—he was a carpenter—Dad would shake down the ashes, through the grate, into the pan and dump them at the side of the house. Every morning he'd hit a clinker or two that stuck in the grate as he moved the handle side to side. A clinker is formed from iron ore embedded in the coal. In the burning, it melts and is fused into strange, distended shapes: amulets, gremlins' toys, saints' relics, fat petunia medallions, iron roses, the Pope's gallstones on Easter morning. Clinkers' little sisters, cinders and ash, were strewn on the driveway.

Books taught me later that diamonds are made of the same element as coal: carbon, another residue of a gone life, subjected to eons of pressure and heat. Diamonds and coal are both fathered by carbon, mothered by earth. Mother holds her diamonds longer, more fiercely, hides them deeper. It is light, refracted through the facets to us that makes the diamond the object of our desire. A stove full of diamonds will yield no warmth.

I was in the first grade when we moved to Centralia, deep in the coal mining country of southern Illinois. That was the year forty-seven miners were buried alive in a cave-in, crushed into a mass grave. The news ran through the little town like a contagion and settled into a deep sadness that colored every day. My father had begun to drift from job to job trying to take hold of a world he never loved. I was afraid he would go down into the mines. He never did.

The buried days stretched into autumn, then into Halloween. I cut my finger on a dime store metal noise maker; the next day it was swollen; by afternoon, a red streak had crossed my palm, crawled onto the wrist, inched up my forearm. Blood poisoning. The doctor told me to soak it in Epsom salts and warm water. I sat at the kitchen table for hours, elbow deep in a porcelain basin. Day after day. Finally, the fire line burning toward my heart began to back down toward my hand, then to fade. Then it was no longer visible. It is still in me somewhere.

Winter closed around us. We lived in a small bare house. One morning Mom gave me a big brown grocery bag and told me to go down to the railroad tracks and fill it with coal. I didn't get it. My folks had warned me never to go near the tracks. *But, Mom . . .. You go on. You'll find coal along the tracks. Bring it home.* When I scrambled down the hillside to the railroad tracks, I began to see other boys walking the edge of the ties, with bags and apple baskets, all searching for coal. Then, the whistle round the bend, the train was slowing, pulling into Centralia, with that throttled chug, chug stroke.

I could see the coal men with their shovels just behind the engine. They spotted us, that gaggle of boys, iron rail beggars, standing in the new cold. I didn't know they were going to do it. Mom did. They began to pitch shovels full of coal for a hundred feet along the edge of the tracks as the train crept past, the man smiling and winking at us as we scrambled to fill our bags and baskets. Stale bread from the king's supper table. Broken body of the Host. I staggered home with my bounty. The bag weighed as much as I did. I got it home.

All things are an exchange of fire: fire unto fire. A diamond ring on a boney finger. Two pieces of coal in a red Christmas stocking. The iron rose blooming in memory. Beneath us, a timber cracks under the weight of a stone sky.

The Maze Walker Meets John Lee Hooker One Last Time

A voice in the dashboard of my rusted out Nova
announces that bluesman John Lee Hooker
has died on this first night of summer.
I sit in the Provincetown Herring Cove parking lot
watching the midnight tide roll in,
listening to the local FM station
play his music hour after hour.

One woman, one bourbon, one scotch, one beer.

I'm gonna ring your doorbell,
knock on your window pane.

Boom, Boom, Boom, Boom.
I'm gonna shoot you right down
right off your feet.

Twenty-five years ago, I hit muddy
bottom in Olney, Illinois, my hometown,
my two-dollar-an-hour job,
packed up whatever I couldn't throw away,
bought a hundred and fifty dollar Buick
from a neighbor and pointed west.
My pop had told me I couldn't pass through
this world without seeing the Rockies,
that the mountain range was visible
on the horizon all the way from Kansas.
I drove straight through and was so
road whacked and Denver so smoggy,
I nearly ran into the Rockies
before I saw them.

***

It was about a hundred degrees.
I got swallowed by the city,

lost in the bowels, hiding out
in refrigerated shithole lounges
till the weather broke.
One beer blurred afternoon, I took up with
a beautiful young Pueblo, a skinny kid,
with a big mane of black hair tied back.
We were swapping stories in a meat
locker basement lounge, everything red,
the walls, the stools, the lights,
drinking Miller beer, the high life,
the champagne of bottled beers,
with that cowgirl vixen smiling,
right at me, on every bottle,
sitting short skirted on the edge
of a quarter moon.
Every label was a get well card
to me, from my girl.

***

The Mazes, he told me I had to go
find the Mazes, in Utah, a crazy, holy place,
where you could be alone with everything,
nobody else within a hundred miles.
One time he was walking the stone corridors,
naked as God made him, picking his way
through the labyrinth, been there for two days,
fasting, purifying his heart, offering
his sadness to something big enough
to swallow it whole.

It was silent in the Mazes, windless,
breathless. Then he began to hear a tiny *sheng*
with each step, a metallic shimmer
like the Kachina dancer's ankle bells.
A step. *Sheng*. He began to dance
in place, surrounded by the silver *sheng*
of ceremonial bells. It wasn't in his head.
It was the music of stone Mazes,

the cut of an old song he'd wandered into,
a song out of the crack between the worlds,
where twilight leaked through,
where the willow bends and bones crack.

Sheng. Sheng. The tiny bells of the Noseless Ones.
His fear was that they would show themselves to him.
He climbed out of the Mazes, never returned,
though he said some days the bells come back,
always behind him.

***

I bought him another Miller, walked over
to the jukebox, plugged in some John Lee Hooker,
that *Crawling King Snake* lost in the dark.

You know you ran away from your home, baby,
And now you want to run away from me too.

The red lounge Pueblo picked up his story:
I saw John Lee Hooker one night here in Denver.
They turned us away at the door.
The guard said they didn't want fucked up Indians in the club.
We were too much trouble, too broke to buy a beer or a ticket.
Six of us went through the bathroom window.
First one in was hard but the rest was easy.
John Lee Hooker played for us all night long.
John Lee Hooker tore that place a new asshole.
Us too.

***

Last thing he told me was how
he wanted to be buried up in the mountains,
higher than the buzzards can fly.
Way to do that, way to dig that grave,
is dynamite, he said. *I spend all my money on beer.*
I can't afford to die.

He was beautiful and crazy, that Pueblo.
Every step he took was mortal.
Every beer was white eyes' blood.
I miss him and wish he'd come through
the bathroom window right now,
lowering himself sprightly to the toilet lid
and to the floor.

Welcome, dynamite brother, I'd say.
Where you been? Grave couldn't hold you?
My kids are grown. My wife is still good lookin'.
And I'm still empty as a gourd most days,
nothin' in me to rattle. I'm afraid God don't love me.
Maybe I don't love him.
I can't hardly walk any more.
I want to go to church but the doors are locked.
Sit down with me. Drink a cold Miller.
Listen to some John Lee Hooker.

I'm a rocking sugar daddy
and I want to rock my baby all night long.

***

I headed straight up over the Rockies,
turned south toward Alamosa,
crossed into New Mexico, through
Eagle Nest and down into Taos.

***

One afternoon I went into the Pueblo village
to pray to the *Santos,* the holy figures in
the little church, to kneel before the Lady of Guadalupe.
Ten years earlier white men had broken
into the church, stolen the statues,
took them to Paris to sell them.
The Pueblos hunted them down all over the world,
brought them back to Taos, back to the church.

Now, there is yellow tape across the aisles,
three rows back from the altar. I knelt there.
Yellow cop tape, crime scene, stay-the-hell
away tape, official tape, murder-been-done-here tape.
Lady of Guadalupe, I cannot kiss your tears.
You cannot kiss mine. I leave my heart
in your keeping.

I walked across the center of the village toward the gate.
A small stream lay ahead, a footpath bridge.
Approaching me was a drunken Pueblo,
much older than the Maze walker,
in an unbuttoned turquoise shirt, a worn man in black pants
with the cowboy cord down the length of the seam.
He danced toward me, an odd side step,
hopping on one foot, the other leg kicked out like a wing.
He came at me across the bridge
gut chanting the word *Yateheh* over and over,
Hello and goodbye in the Tiwa dialect of the Pueblo.

His hand was extended, palm up.
I offered him change from my pockets,
then dollars.
He refused both.
When he got close to me, I saw
that his left boot was full of blood.
I could hear it squish as he danced a circle around me.
Yateheh. Yateheh.
Whatever he wanted, I didn't have.
He offered something I didn't know
how to take from him.
I didn't cross that narrow, rickety bridge.
He danced away and gone.

***

Now I know he wanted me
to kick my crutches away
and dance toward him,

dance my own crazy, drunken blood
across that narrow footbridge,
to follow him home,
sit with his wife and children at their table,
lose myself in their prayers,
to swap my left shoe for his bloody boot.

Yateheh. Yateheh.
Anywhere on this earth,
hello and *goodbye* in the same breath.

All the Way to Heaven Is Heaven

Saint Catherine of Siena

I have never believed in the evolution
of the old world,
the notion that all of this is unfolding,
growing upward like the branches of a tree,
up into heaven, into a hollow sky
we call home.

I like it here, right here.
As far as I can tell
none of this is going anywhere.
If there is movement at all,
my life is turning in on itself.
There is nowhere to go.

We are all members of one body,
though broken into pieces,
though broken into pieces,
though broken into pieces.
The Kingdom of Heaven
gladly suffers violence
from hot love
and living hope.

For My Mother Beatrice Summers on Her 90th Birthday

The first hard freeze comes tonight,
December 5, the evening of your 90th birthday.
We have cut the last of the roses
and set them in little vases,
asking them to stay a while longer.
Never have they bloomed this late
into the season.

The hardiest of the dozens of roses
around our house is the Tamora,
a pale pink blossom that has refused to wilt
in the frosts, break in the winds
or yield to blight.
Its fragrance is a celestial vanilla,
painted with honey-hammered ginger.
In another time, you might have been named Tamora.

You have stayed late with us.
The days grow short.
The snow will come soon.

You remain, as I have always known you,
in bloom in a world broken yet whole,
in bloom in the pale sunlight of late fall,
in bloom wherever you find yourself planted,
my dear mother, my December rose.

Knock upon Yourself as upon a Door for the First Time

Light, powdery snow drifts outside the window. Today's *Cleveland Plain Dealer* talks to me, page 3A, national news—big black letters: *North Pole Could Melt by the End of this Century.* That will be it for Santa Claus and his sleigh and his reindeer. I wonder when the last snowflake will fall, as the earth heats up. Who will see that last snowflake and will they kneel to catch that final snowflake on the tip of the tongue. And what will we make of that person's passing? Headline: *The Last Person to See a Snowflake Dies at Age of 107.* Some will remember stories of obese snow creatures, with carrot noses and anthracite eyes, tree branch arms, legless, silent creatures who were sacrificed to a burning star. After a time, the stories themselves will be forgotten and will be supplanted by effigies of stone and by holy lava marking the brow of the faithful.

For the past week, I have been traveling to the mountain. It is not far. Go down route 43 here in Kent, about a mile south of downtown. Take a right into the University Plaza parking lot. Look just behind Katie's Corner ice cream shop. There is the mountain. All the parking lot snow bulldozed into a pile the size of a Greyhound bus. The snow mountain presents itself as a concealment, one of its lessons: so much is hidden and what is hidden is near.

Out of the snow peak protrudes the black rubber tire of an abandoned shopping cart; on the slope the red handle of another cart is barely visible. A blue ski glove, mashed soda cans, water bottles and on the east slope a women's black blouse. I circle the mountain slowly in my car, lean out the window. I search for whatever might have punched through the veil: a swami's hourglass, Custer's golden scalp, Penelope's frosted mango panties, the talking parrot who rattles off the name of every bone in the human body. I long to come across the glass eye of Polyphemus. I want to see what he saw, the shadows on the cave wall. Oh, mountain, show me the chains the freed man left behind. The empty silver lipstick tube after all the sweet kisses have been given away.

Last Tuesday when the temperature hit 70 degrees, I sat in the car for half an hour and watched a bright stream of melted snow sparkle its way across the asphalt, to a grated storm drain a hundred feet away. It will take many years, decades, but finally that stream will cut its way through the asphalt and down into the earth to rejoin the water table upon which all our dinners are set.

Yesterday, a light new snow as fine as chalk dust covered the mountain range. It is smaller each time I return. Everything is going away. We know that. Everything falls under the law of transformation. Water is not snow. Snow is not water. Each is a transformation of the other. They don't look alike but they share an essential nature. None of us looks like a sperm wiggling its way into a microscopic egg. That bulldozed mountain of snow, what is it? The birth of an ocean-bound river? The bright killing field of winter? A cemetery for torched snow people?

The soul may not be inside the body; nor out in the world. Perhaps we can find it where the inner and outer worlds touch one another. We search for it all our lives, wandering river banks, building towers of stone, drinking the blood of gods and eating their flesh, pledging our loves, in trust, digging among ruins, piecing together the words of a lost language. Always seek the place of touching, skin to skin, earth to sky, ink to page, snow to asphalt.

Pour the black waters into the white china cup. Spill the black ink onto the snowfield of the days. At the heart of that cold mountain, there is a music that wells from strings no fingers have ever touched. Listen hard for that.

Salt

The autumnal equinox arrives Saturday morning, 11:44. Equinox, equal night, equal day. The sun appears to cross the celestial equator at that point, north to south. For a moment, everything is in balance. The crooked is made straight. The cradle stops rocking. Summer departs; fall is ushered in. Voluptuous summer in a green gown sadly shuffles away, pestered by a skinny old piker in a mottled coat. We measure everything: seasons, years, hours, millennia, teaspoons, tons, time. We cannot live in an unmeasured world.

My Old Man told me that at the exact moment of equinox it is possible to stand a raw egg on its end. He explained that in that instant, since the equator and the sun were on the same plane, the equator ran right through the egg, like an axis. It made sense to me at the time. He carefully stood the egg on the kitchen table and slowly moved his hands away. There it was, in perfect equipoise. A small astonishment.

It was not until my teens, after his magical act had finally failed and the egg rolled across the table and plopped on the floor, that Pop confessed that it had been a trick all along. He had prearranged a little pile of salt on the white tablecloth and set the egg down in it, waving his hands like a swami, like a priest at liturgy, as a distraction. Salt. The answer is salt. But, I never got over the need to believe in the mystical nature of the equinox. I have made too much of this, but that is how I want to live. Everything in me believes that in that moment between breaths, an unseen hand nudges us awake and holds us upright, the equator running right through us from head to heel, holding us in perfect balance and clarity, the dervish stopped in full spin. In that instant, all the world's brokenness is repaired. All suffering ceases.

Tomorrow morning, when that hushed moment comes, stack your armor, hold your breath, empty your head and see what happens. Perhaps a Luna moth will brush the back of your neck and your heart will crash land in the Sea of Tranquility. Or you will hear the iron church bells playing with the wind a hundred miles away. Maybe you will find yourself standing knee deep in the riffles of Time's cold, muddy river.

If you do stand on your head in a pile of salt, do it barefoot, so you can translate the starlight psalms with the soles of your feet. Don't worry. You won't topple over.

One of the answers has always been salt.

Lake Shining

Spring deepens. After a night of hard rain, the day breaks open into a fresh, cornflower blue with shards of cloud. I am out early on the back porch, coffee and these lines from an Aztec poem. *That we come to this earth to live is untrue: we come but to sleep, to dream.* I watch the birds at the feeders. A dusty goldfinch, a female, solitary, pecking at thistle. A house finch, blush of red from brow to breast. Two chickadees, chattering at one another, delighted and abuzz. A hummingbird darts from fir tree to sugar water feeder, then perches on the clothes line, staring at my dreaming. These are the day's entries, the back yard post parade.

I do some mojo calculations on the *Daily Racing Form* for Thistledown and find a play. I call in my bet from my back porch, telephone account betting. I have found my way to turn the dharma wheel. The sixth race, one mile, that honest distance, for $7500 claimers, three years old and upward who have never won two races, nine horses going to the post. It comes down to three horses. Throw out the others. *Lake Shining* is dropping in class, from a $10,000 claimer last time out. He draws the one hole, has enough early foot to get a good position entering the first turn. I am drawn to *Crown of Glory* who broke his maiden at this distance, showed a middle move last race and is coming back in nine days, a sign his trainer thinks he is ready. *Great Deception* just missed by a neck last time out, nine days ago. Any horse coming back in less than ten days is worth a look, particularly if that last race was a game effort. The clincher is that *Great Deception* is switching to a frontline jockey, Heriberto Rivera, Jr., plus his speed figures show me he is getting better, a 58 last time out.

I play a one-dollar trifecta box, six bucks total. The horses come in 1/4/5. Kicking back $112.90. I made a hundred dollars today and never left the sanctuary of my back porch, protected by winged creatures and the shields of flowers. This is the job I want.

Lake Shining
Crown of Glory
Great Deception

That order and no other. Shining/Glory/Deception. The filling and the spilling of the cup. Stations marking a journey across a desert. The raising up. The blazing into light. The undoing. A map to freedom tattooed on the left shoulder of a prisoner.

The poet Dan Bourne on living in Warsaw. He says the souls of the dead never left the city after the war ended and Poland was freed. En masse, they hover over Warsaw, tethered to what they cannot leave, a roiling cloud of leaden spirit. Some days, you can see them, gathered in the dark sky, hear their voices in the wind.

One midnight my wife LuAnn and I were floating in the mountain hot springs, the alpine plain, six thousand feet, Burgdorf, Idaho, the mist climbing into the cold air, floating naked in one another's arms. It came from the north, cylindrical with a half dozen lighted portals, inching its way across the Milky Way. It paused over us. It was the sky ship of the Nez Perce fathers, the old men with dry groins, the lodge keepers, come to look down on us. This was their country, all the way to the Canadian border, a land they fought so bitterly to keep. Lu and I held on to one another, looking up, buoyed by the mineral water as salty as tears. The faces of the fathers withdrew from the windows. The ship moved off to the south, leaving us to what is to come—the shining, the glory, the deception. The fathers look down on a world once theirs. The souls above Warsaw moan.

The Hat

That old man I saw years ago at Thistledown race track, sitting solitary while the patrons hustled around him. He had found a chair up against a pillar inside the grandstand and was buried in the Daily Racing Form. He must have been eighty or so, turkey necked, a red radish bulbous nose, toothless, his shirt front besotted with mustard, the dog long gone, crooked glasses perched on that wall banger schnoz. He was all bundled up in a worn tweed topcoat in which he carried most of what was his, old racing programs rolled and stuffed in every pocket. He was a penitent, one of God's old children loitering at the Gate.

On his head, a black ball cap with this red satin stitched credo across the front: SO MANY WOMEN, SO LITTLE TIME. It was a brand new hat. I was on my way to the window when I passed him. When I came back, the old coot was gone. So little time. I was dead set on making him an offer for that hat, whatever it took. I didn't care if it fit because I could never wear it. Except maybe alone around the house. Or in a foreign country where I was sure no one could read English. And I wouldn't put it on the hat deck of my car so folks behind me could chuckle at it. It is nothing to chuckle about. Love and Time. That daily double we all play. Love in Time. Love on Time. Will I have Time to Love enough? It is what your checkout girl is thinking about when she brushes the bar code past the magic eye, what your mailman is lost in when he drops your letters in the box and walks away, what the cop is really chewing on when he writes that ticket. You make up the rest.

I doubt that old track rat bought it for himself or that he plays on a slow-pitch softball team named SO MANY WOMEN, SO LITTLE TIME, sponsored by a local funeral home. Maybe it was a gag gift by a wise ass, gone wrong son-in-law. I have never seen another like it, this double edged sword of mortality and longing. The hat I do see, the one most fellas wear, carries the inscription SO FEW WOMEN, SO MUCH TIME. My hunch is that most of the guys who wear that hat don't know they have it on. Nobody gives you that hat. It sort of grows on you, little by little, till it becomes visible, like the gray in your hair. That old dilemma: you can see everyone else's hat but you can't see your own. Sometimes, in John Barleycorn's grand arena, on the barstools of the world, those hats will line up for as far as you can see, all with the same baleful epitaph across the front, SO FEW WOMEN, SO MUCH TIME, with no woman within a country mile.

I'll bet I never see him again, that old dry-balls duffer at the racetrack with those red letters proclaiming his fate . . . SO MANY WOMEN, SO LITTLE TIME. When I pass that empty chair, I'll remember that here sat one of the Immortals, a man who had broken the code and found the truth in a string of six words. And if we stumble across one another again, old Daddy Sawbucks eaten away by the years, may I find you with Dolly Parton sitting on your Rocky Top lap, arms round your neck, whispering winner after winner in your ear, her honey suckle musk breath singeing your whiskers.

So many women, so little time. Maybe the oldest graffiti in the world. Remember, you old rascal, that's my hat.

On the Road to Mandalay

Today, March 18, is my father's birthday, Daniel Wayne Ragain, born 1916, died 1990. He would have been ninety five. He was born a minute after St. Patty's Day, a secret regret all his life. An Irishman missed his saint's day by a minute. *Too late my brothers, but never mind. All my sorrows soon be over.* I've inherited some of that too-late stuff. I won't offer an inventory, but I know what it is.

It was my Pop, along with my home school teacher, Effie Eberhardt, who first opened the door to poetry for me. He did some hard time as a carpenter and a construction worker, building things for other people. He fixed the little things in his life and turned away from the big ones. He kept his thoughts and feelings to himself, a solitary man, but now and then at the supper table, on the back porch overlooking the lake, after he had been emptied by the day, he would begin to drift and talk. One evening, he asked me how my home schooling was going with the teacher who visited each weekday afternoon. I was twelve or so. I told him we had studied a poem by someone named Kipling. It was about a faraway land named Mandalay. There were so many words I didn't know. *When Mrs. Eberhardt read it aloud, Pop, it seemed so sad.* His face brightened.

In a quiet firm voice I'd never heard before, he turned his eyes to the lake and said,

> *By the old Moulmein Pagoda, lookin' lazy at the sea,*
> *There's a Burma girl a settin', and I know she thinks o' me;*
> *for the wind is in the palm-trees, and the temple bells they say:*
> *Come you back, you British Soldier, come you back to*
> *Mandalay.*

> *Come you back to Mandalay,*
> *Where the old flotilla lay:*
> *Can't you 'ear their paddles chunkin' from Rangoon to*
> *Mandalay.*

On the road to Mandalay,
Where the flyin' fishes play,
And the dawn comes up like thunder out of China
Crost the bay.

My mother sat still as a Buddha, her hands in her lap, staring at Pop. My little brother Michael held his fork halfway to his mouth. Young as I was, somehow I sensed that the Burma girl a sittin' reminded Pop of someone he had known in his youth and would never see again. Mom must have figured that out too. He was so tender with the words. I didn't know he could feel that way. That Pop knew those lines just didn't make any sense. I'd never seen him read anything other than a carpenter's manual, a newspaper or a detective magazine. That last stanza...*On the road to Mandalay,* those four lines . . . found its way so deep inside me that, to this day, I hear it in my head at the oddest times, in the car at a stop light, dropping into sleep, watching a river run. Always it is Pop's voice.

It was my first taste of the enduring life of poetry, how it can link what is here with the past, how scratchings on a page can come alive, how that voice extends far beyond our brief time. It was my first inkling that my father had a secret, inner life I'd never know. Later, I came to believe that everyone has such a life and that we are each alone with that.

There are no flyin' fishes in that little lake in southeastern Illinois. The road to Mandalay still beckons, though I'll never travel it, and the Burma girl is still waiting, as we all are, for someone and something. My father climbed the long ladder of poetry up out of himself, took me with him to that *Old Moulmein Pagoda* and showed me his heart.

On the road to Mandalay
Where the flyin' fishes play
And the dawn comes up like thunder out of China
Crost the bay.

To My Son, from Greece

Alton, Illinois, Memorial Hospital. You were born there, 1964. I was held there, in 1947, burned up by polio, that nerve eating fever. They took me there from the Centralia quarantine ward. I was seven years old. A nurse carried me in her arms, out to a long gray car, and lay me down in the back seat for the trip to Alton. I didn't know, or care, where I was going, I remember I was afraid my butt would hang out, but I was too weak to fix it. She was a big woman and carried me against her breast, *humpf, humpf,* as we walked out into the fresh air. It must have been September. Someone covered me with an Army blanket. We crossed rivers, the steel girders against the sky, the wash of leaves under the car.

In Centralia, the therapy of choice had been the hot packs. The hot packs were the inspiration of one Sister Kenny, an Australian nun, who revolutionized the treatment of polio patients. The hot packs consisted of flannel cloths which had been steamed in what looked like stainless steel lobster vats. The packs were lifted from the steamers with tongs, then wrapped around my legs and body. Plastic was quickly layered over the flannel to keep the steam in, then safety pinned. This was believed to rejuvenate the muscle and nerve.

One day, a documentary film crew wheeled their cameras and lights to my bedside. The orderlies rolled in the hot steamers and the hot packs. Lights. Cameras. Action. This time I wouldn't do it. When the cameras rolled, I told them how badly it hurt. I couldn't find words for how little I believed in Sister Kenny, no sister of mine, with her hot packs from heaven and how, even as a child, I believed they should have listened to my small voice, that they owed me what I would later understand as the integrity of my solitude. I cried out. They had to stop the filming. Everyone was pissed at me for days, in a tight lipped way. I was the kid who ruined Sister Kenny's March of Dimes and Dollars inspirational film. Why couldn't I be quiet when the lights were on? The question persists. When the big nurse in Centralia carried me out into the fresh autumn air, I was quiet.

In Alton Memorial, I had a room with a big window that cranked out, ground floor. My mother would come to the window and talk to me after visiting hours. She brought gifts from the world outside, a watch I wouldn't wear, oranges I wouldn't eat . . . and then one afternoon a Classic Comic book, *Black Arrow.* That I ate and all the others, *Gulliver's Travels, David Copperfield, The Tale of Two Cities,* the whole library.

After lights-out in the ward, I rose from my bed as a man in an iron mask, a man who stood two years before the mast, unrepentant as the cat o' nine tails drew blood. Uncas and I were the last of the Mohicans, slipping down the dark hospital halls and out into the night, Sister Kenny's bloody scalp dangling from my belt. It revealed to me, for the first time, those who didn't have to die, those with small bones, big feathers, who live on through the appetites of others, who mark trails, who sleep safe in treetops. I heard what I believed was my own heart in the world.

They put me in the tubs of warm water and Epsom salts, but no more hot packs. There weren't enough tubs, so mostly I stayed in bed, read the classics and listened to the radio. That winter of '48, there was one song that never went away. I sang it. It sang me. I'd turn the dial till I found it. Nights, when the hospital ward was dark and quiet, I imagined myself as a Morse Code operator in a submarine, scanning for signals, rigged for silent running. That's how I want to be rigged.

Up in the morning, out on the job, work like a devil for my pay, but that lucky old sun got nothin' to do but roll around heaven all day. I'd sing myself to sleep with it. I wanted to be free that way, to be lucky and roll around everything, the world, heaven. That is how I want to be with you. I want to roll around you, not wrap you up, just roll around you, my lucky breath on your neck.

Finally, I got strong enough to sit on the edge of the bed. The nurses would steady me and take their hands away. One day I sat there, unattended, an amazement, perched on the edge. Then, I'd do it myself, up on my elbows, swing around and up. I'd sit there and count the minutes. And, though I was just a kid, I began to know in those days that my life was coming back to me, that the black arrow could never pierce my heart, that I had friends in the unseen who watched over me. I could close my eyes and feel them touch my shoulders.

My folks came to take me home in the late winter. There was an argument between the doctors and Mom and Dad about what was best. It is hard to contend with tall men in starched white coats who fill their mouths with words like rehabilitation and motor skills. My folks made the final appeal: they made the doctors acknowledge the authority of the parents' love for a child. The drawbridge was lowered, and I went home.

My father had no work. We moved in with my grandmother, Blanche Goldie Totten, 401 West Chestnut in Olney. My father set up my red and white Schwinn bicycle on a wooden stand, its rear wheel elevated, the frame steadied. He carried me in his arms and bid me sit on the narrow seat and pedal. I couldn't do it. I could feel my feet, but they wouldn't move. He was a carpenter and a millwright and a man who understood tolerances and I miss him. It won't do you any good to look up the word tolerances in the dictionary.

You, Sean, were born sixteen years later, in the green afternoon, May 29, 1964, in Alton Memorial Hospital. It was a long labor. Your mother cried out. I was barricaded in the waiting room with a Pepsi truck driver. We both chain smoked Pall Malls and feared the moment. I was afraid you and Carole would die. My heart feared the world would not tolerate love, that, though the word was in everyone's mouth, those who gave themselves to love were scattered, ashes to the winds. But, they rolled you out, in your mother's arms, on the gurney, your eyes squinted against the new light, black knot at your belly, cheesecake at every wrinkle. It took me a year to pay you off, six hundred and seventy one dollars. Easy money.

Tonight, a dark trench of water holds the continents and the two of us apart. Quit your job. Come to Greece. I'll pick up the one way ticket. We'll drink Amstel and retsina for breakfast and talk baseball all day in the tavernas. Remember when you and I went up to Cleveland Stadium to watch the Dutchman, Bert Blyleven, pitch? The stories won't go away, how when he first came into the American League, his curve ball was so tight and nasty that batters said they could hear it break over the plate? Could hear it. Sean, it is the same sound the olive trees make when they break into blossom down in the Peloponnese. Come. Let's roll around. Let's listen. Together. It is opening day again.

I Want to Sing an Old, Old Song

The caretakers of the golden calf,
convening at the long oak table,
that chopping block, send down word:
abandon my watch as a part-time
temporary employee and I may now claim
what is due me: a monthly bucket brimful
of quarters, with an annual index adjustment,
guaranteed for as long as I can live.

I have made my own provisions,
knowing it would come to this.
Lean toward me.
Brush my cheek with your hair.
In the palm of my hand
find a small map of the soul.
It is difficult to read.
There are no boundaries,
townships or longitude.
The colors are primary, corpuscular.
Here, red does not mean stop,
green go.

The heart line is a broken trail
The line of life splits off
toward a warped knuckle.
In the palm's midwest,
a bearded man has staked out
a dog behind his house.
It has walked a bare dirt ring
into the grass.

All this belongs to me.
Understand it as a merriment,
an ignition in a dark place,
where the soul sets its table.

Letter to America, from Ta Pham Duy Tien

A response to Handicapped Children's Wishes,
a crayon drawing by Ta Pham Duy Tien,
Vietnam, age thirteen.

I want you to look at me.
Look at my brother.
I have no hands, no arms.
From him, the land mines
stole an arm, a leg.
We are the children whose father is war.

My brother hops from step to step
on his one leg. He steadies himself on my small shoulder.
I will not leave his side.
He dreams of flying away among the stars.
I dream of teaching the children.

I am scribbling this with a crayon
gripped between my toes.
When you have learned
to scrawl your own words this way,
I hope you will reply to this letter.

Tell me and my brother why.
Why the bombs, the mines, the fire jelly napalm,
how we became your enemy.

Touch us with a part of you
that has been severed from you.
Then you will understand.

Living Day to Day Is Never What It Seems

Oh, Daniel,
what is this life we share
in snow and cold and hope,
barren trees and drums,
poems and hostage hearts,
and the body's secret life,
midnight accordions,
the grief of widows,
pale sunlight on an oak table,
a window facing west.

Stone Song, Dollars in the Jar

Raising Money for Daniel Thompson's Gravestone,
at the Algebra Tea House, Feb. 12, 2005

A stone tablet, chiseled name, 1935-2004, the page unturned.

A stone, slicked with cold rain, pointing the way.

A stone-bare knuckle in the city fathers' bone yard.

A stone porch light welcoming back the wanderer, the front
door unlatched.

A stone moon circling our years, waxing, waning.

A stone poem, broken haiku, scattered letters, silent drums.

A stone accordion, busted bellows, too heavy for one man.

A stone for Daniel's slingshot against the Giant.

A stone anchor, rope cut, the boat adrift on the ebb tide.

A worry stone worn smooth by an unseen thumb.

A stone for the black iron soup kettle to feed the street
sleepers.

A stone tulip, rusted brown, in a garden of gray stones.

A stone heart that beats once every year, daybreak, death
break, May 6th.

A stone upon which to sharpen grief, that silver blade, to a
sliver, then gone.

A stone in the Lakeview cemetery Stonehenge, keeper of the
solstice.

Name It What You Will

My father and I were walking along Fox Creek, behind my grandparents' farm, southeastern Illinois. I was six years old. Dad was a year out of the Marine Corps. It was 1946. Dad carried a bundle of cane poles under his arm, working his way toward our fishing hole. I followed, staying close, on the slippery bank. We came to a small stream entering the river, about five feet across, shallow, sandy bottom. Dad hesitated a moment, then stepped into the middle of the stream.

In a blink, he was in up to his thighs, then thrashed from side to side. Dad grabbed at a tree limb to steady himself. I can still see his eyes. The deep-blue clouded, clabbered over, as if his vision suddenly had turned inward. Name it what you will. He finally struggled over on his belly, holding fast to a tree root, then pulled one leg out with a slurp suck sound. Then the other. He sat up across from me, on the other side of the little stream, put his hands on his knees and breathed heavily.

Quicksand, nodding at what had nearly swallowed him. He walked up the bank and circled back round to me. I stood and stared at the stream that looked only six inches deep, muddied, but no trace of what had happened. I remember thinking it seemed oddly alive, hungry, placid, awake, waiting. We never got to the fishing hole, the deep cut by the downed Oak. Dad spoke only once, as we walked across the pasture toward the farmhouse. *The more you struggle, the quicker you go.*

It is a story in one word. Quicksand. Years later, in the Saturday afternoon movies at the Elks theater in Olney, featuring Tarzan, the ape man, or Sabu, the jungle boy, every now and then, a quicksand scene would come to life. Usually the villain was in pursuit when he plunged in. It played out in slow minutes as Mr. Bad went under, clutching at this and that, futilely, as he begged and suffered. Often the Pursued, the Good, the Saved, would come back and offer a tree branch or rope. It never worked. Evil Doers are punished. The Good are redeemed. Simple as that. There was usually a confession or some kind of fitting signoff before the quicksand closed over his head, and he began the long descent to the bottom, littered with bones and skulls. Then the long steady camera shot as the pockmark closed and it looked, once again, like nothing more than a patch of muddy ground.

I always had to turn away from those moments. There was Dad again, going down into that awful cold clutch, looking hard at me, pleading with me to save him, to forgive him, his blue eyes, scudded with cloud, the light leaving those eyes. Sixty years later, I still cannot watch one of those scenes, though I know his life didn't end that way.

He died on his kitchen tile floor of a massive stroke, solid ground at least. If the quicksand had taken him that summer day on the Fox Creek, what could I have done? How could I have gone on with my life? Dad would have been lost in a nameless place, one of those secret grottoes the living cannot enter, one of those dark worlds inside this world, from which none returns.

The Anguish That Lives inside Steel

A siren rushes by, up Route 43,
a half block from my house,
headed north, in pursuit of a rescue,
a heart stopped mid beat, flames eating at a house,
a crime at gunpoint, a splintered windshield
and twisted steel, a birth strangled.

The siren, the banshee, calls with the news
we never want to hear. The siren luring
the sailors into the rocks, the boat
breaking apart on an anvil of stone.
The siren, metallic, full throated,
revved-up scream, the anguish that lives
inside steel, born in the foundry's hell.

The siren, a mother, her arms clasped
against her breast, kneels beside
the body of her only child, keening.
The siren gnashes with metal teeth:

Hear my song. Fear me.
Fear God as I pass by.

The Small Red Ball

At Zelma's Collectibles, Penn Yan, New York, a white-haired woman, blue and white house dress, is seated behind the counter. *Welcome*, she says, in a distracted way, staring at what looks like a cube of wooden clothes pins at the center of which is imprisoned a small red ball. *It's a kid's puzzle*, she says. *I've been working on it for hours. I can't get the ball out. It's for kids*, I tell her, *You'd better surrender.*

Her name is *Marla May. Marla May Or Marla May Not. That's what I call myself.* She grins. I'm about to tell her my name is *Mares Eat Oats And Does Eat Oats* and I got a wife who calls herself *Little Lambs Eat Ivy*, but I don't want to be a smart ass and get in the way of what might come next. I'm checking out the old pocket knives when she begins to tell me her story.

I come from north of here, around Dundee, the Irish, lots of potato fields, poor folks. My father was a carpenter. I was raised in a little shack, no running water, no electricity, with an outhouse. My father was a jokester; inside that outhouse, he rigged up a fake porcelain water tank with a flush handle. City folks would traipse out back for a sit down, then come back complaining that, no matter how many times they tried, the darned toilet wouldn't flush. He never told them. He woke up every morning hoping for company.

I owed her one. A tale about my own childhood adventures with my grandparents' outhouse, in the mid nineteen forties, back in farm country Illinois. I was about five, a bib overalls peewee, with an early flair for trouble. The outhouse was a two seater at the back of the chicken yard, a lengthy hike from the backdoor, with reason. In the long, hot summers, it grew unbearably fragrant. In the winters, it was, hands down, the coldest place on God's earth. The toilet paper was crinkly one ply, pages torn from a Montgomery Ward catalog (Monkey Ward, my grandma called it), if you were lucky, corn cobs if not. The first and last rule: don't look down.

My own outhouse undoing came about when the Totten boys and I decided to do some butt peeking around back where a zinc roofing sheet had been pulled away just enough. It offered us a bull's-eye view of the two-round sit-down holes. We held our noses and waited. (By now, Marla May Or Marla May Not has put down the puzzle and picked up my story.) The squeaky hinged door opened and banged shut. A shuffle and a butt appeared. Then, the door again. Another butt settled in. A double butt score. Two split watermelons.

It was more than we could take. One of us snickered and bumped the zinc sheeting. Gone were the butts. The door flew open. It was Grandpa Chester and Grandma Blanche. The three ornery pups tried to light out for the territory, but we didn't get far. Grandma tore a switch from the willow and got me good on the back of both legs. Grandpa chased Don and Pat half way across the barnyard and sent them up the road.

We never told anyone that we'd been butt watching for weeks. We were never sure how many different people had come and gone because honestly all butts kind of look the same from that angle. I didn't tell that part to Marla May Or Marla May Not because I didn't want to step over the line. I knew I'd never be here with her again. And this other thing had started unfolding along with the stories.

I had begun to see her worn face changing, little by little, in the half hour that we burned together, something inward slowly birthing the beautiful young woman she had once been, as a rose emerges from the bud, as the muscles of the petals open to the world. She was blooming, growing more lovely by the minute, right in front of me. I am not making it up. I knew it wouldn't make any sense to Marla May Or Marla May Not were I to tell her. I am not sure it will make sense to you.

I felt blessed and a little crazy at the thought that this might happen with every old person I saw, that I would live in a circus of transformations so intense that one day I wouldn't be able to recognize anyone. No one would believe me. Finally, I would be all alone, adrift in a nameless place. I closed my eyes. I couldn't look anymore.

I paid for a couple of treasures, a purple silk Indian purse and a yellow African hat, nothing I needed or wanted, the price of admission. Marla May Or Marla May Not wrote a receipt on a yellow sales slip. *Blessings*, I nodded and, as I left the shop, I turned to ask, *Do you want to send that little red ball puzzle out the door with me? That would solve it.*

No, she said, *I can do it*. The last words of Marla May Or Marla May Not. *No, I can do it*, calling to me from that sea of roses in which, even now, I long to drown.

Those Who Watch Over Our Sleep and Solitude

I am sitting in the late-spring sunshine,
its slant over the trees.
I can hear the river, the Cuyahoga,
its gray spirit running toward the lake.
I am learning to return
to my country after my exile
in Greece. I close my eyes.
I can hardly stay in this body.

A man walks through my head, up to my table,
as he did in Thessaloniki, an Albanian beggar,
down from the mountains, from that country
of cold mud and two flashlights.
A child is trundled on his back,
a small girl asleep.
He begins to play a tin whistle, softly.
He does not want to wake the child.
I dip my hands in whiskey
and hold it to his mouth.
He plays. The child sleeps. I listen.

Everything I want to tell you
about my being here with you
is in this poem.

Look at me. I'll say it again.
He plays. The child sleeps.

IV

Know that the heart makes its home
where it must.

Hammer on the Roof, Morning Meditation

This morning I struggle to sit in bent meditation,
holding fast to the words *thy will*, over and over.
The words drift ahead in the field of vision,
careening around corners, in flight.
Thy will. I follow the tail lights.
The landscape tilts. *Thy will.*
The motion finally slows after
a quarter of an hour. My breath slows. *Thy will.*
Two beats. *Thy will.* Two beats. *Thy will.*
Bam. Bam.

A third beat enters. *Bam. Bam. Bam.*
Spark of things remembered.
It is my father, the carpenter, laying shingles
on our roof, the lake cottage, fifty years ago.
I am a child in the house, listening.
Always three beats, three strikes with the hammer.
The last harder, flattening the nail head on the shingle.

He holds the nails between his lips,
a tailor with his straight pins. Sewing his shroud.
Bam. Bam. Bam. Three beats of his heart.
Under my breath, out into the emptiness without bounds,
I make mantra of my father's hammer strikes
above me. *Bam. Bam. Bam.*

Under the Guidance of Falling Petals

Polio burned its way through me in August of 1948, just as I was ready to start the fourth grade at Central School, Olney, Illinois. Poliomyelitis. Infantile Paralysis. The fear of every parent. Lethargy, thirst, fever. A spinal tap confirmed Bulbar Polio, the mean strain of virus, the worm that ate the apple. A year in hospitals, therapy, then home. Full length metal leg braces. A flak jacket back brace. A let's-push-him-around high-back wooden wheelchair. I was nine years old, a slight, pale boy with a head full of blue sky and muddy river, an arrow frozen in mid-flight.

Illinois state law stipulated that my education be continued. Education, from the Latin *Educio*, to be led forth, that I might enter society as a responsible and productive citizen and find my place in history. The Richland county school board deemed that I be visited by a teacher for two hours each weekday afternoon. I didn't want to be visited by anyone. I couldn't meet people's eyes the first time they saw me. I was safe in my room, dreaming, listening to the radio, riding the airwaves on my bed, that small boat, whispering adventures to myself.

Most days, I thought of myself as a pirate, the first stirrings of a secret life, a kind of movie screen inside my head. A buccaneer. A swashbuckler. I came across that word and I loved to whisper it, a threat, a promise. *Swashbuckler, swashbuckler.* A man of action who could buckle your swash if you weren't careful, who lived by his own laws and took what he wanted. I flew the skull and crossbones. My country tis of thee I sing. My beard was blue. My heart was black. I didn't want any visitors to my hideaway where I sat alone amidst the plunder, my cutlass stashed 'neath my bed.

That first school day in September, I waited for the teacher to arrive. I couldn't figure out how to present myself, where to sit, how to meet her eyes, what to say. To this day that plagues me. Finally, I decided to take off my braces and sit on the bed, to lean against the wall for support, my skinny legs tucked under me, just a regular fella at ease with himself and the world. I practiced what to say, *Oh, hello*, in an off-hand way, not giving away much but acting both pleased and surprised to see her. I'd seen adults pull this off.

I heard her car in the gravel driveway. I peeked out from behind the curtain. The car was light blue, shiny, maybe new, nothing like that in this lakeside neighborhood of patched-up summer cottages. What if she was a well-to-do town lady who would scoff at our little lives? I flushed as Mom greeted her kindly at the front door and brought her to my room where I sat like a bump on a log. *Major, this is Miss Effie Eberhardt. She is going to be your teacher. Oh, hello*, I muttered, my gaze reading the floor.

Effie was maybe forty, prematurely gray, unmarried, on the brink of becoming an old maid, a woman of independent resolve who belonged to herself and no other. She was, as Mom put it, *fixity*—that is, one who spent time and care fixing herself up (not down), love's red rose lipstick, hair carefully spray-shaped, bejeweled eyeglasses she sometimes wore around her neck on a silver chain, the tasteful blush of rouge. She never wore a house dress, rather one of those movie star Loretta Young full-skirted pleated bells that crinkled and tolled as she sat down on the edge of my bed to begin the day's instruction. I had never met anyone like her. She loved the pages of books and tasted words as if they were food that sustained her life, the alphabet soup, the ink broth.

One day, she read aloud a poem by Vachel Lindsay who was born and raised in Springfield, Illinois, two or three hours north of Olney. He was a minstrel, a wanderer, a free man with a great broken heart. His poem was titled *The Leaden-Eyed*.

> *Let not young souls be smothered out*
> *before they do quaint deeds and fully flaunt their pride.*
> *It is the world's one great crime*

its babes grow dull, its poor
are limp, ox-like and leaden-eyed.

Not that they starve, but starve so dreamlessly.
Not that they sow, but seldom reap.
Not that they serve, but have no gods to serve.
Not that they die, but that they die like sheep.

This wasn't the dull-fear talk that I was beginning to hear all around me, the talk that wants to diminish us and tether us to the world of things. The voice in this poem, not Effie but Lindsay, was calling me out, challenging me not to starve dreamlessly, to awaken and stay awake. I felt its truth in my breastbone. And Lindsay had found a way for the poem to hold the meaning, as a hive holds honey. I have returned to this poem till I know it by heart. I say it aloud at odd moments, as a way of summoning courage, remembering what I must do, to dream, to serve, to sow. I didn't think in these terms at eleven or so, but when I read that poem now, more than fifty years later, I can still hear what I heard then. I can dip my tin cup in that clear, shining water—different water, same river—my first sense that there is something imperishable and boundless in what we do, saved inside words.

More poems. They stirred in me a sense of my small life adrift, in an immense world, the currents carrying me toward Tierra del Fuego, the Bering Straits, Antarctica. I wandered nightly outward from my room, following the whale paths, intrepid little brother of Amerigo Vespucci, of Vasco de Gama, brave men who rode out the storms' rage. I wandered across the name of an oasis in central Algeria SSE of Bechar—Reggan. Ragain, my last name. Had my ancestors made lives there? One night, I knelt and drank from that oasis spring while a sandstorm gathered on the horizon. I rode my Bedouin stallion just ahead of the harrowing storm, galloping into our neighborhood just before daybreak, setting free the stallion and slipping into my bed just before Dad got up to make coffee.

I became stronger on my crutches, less time in the chair. I'd walk laps around the little circle driveway by the house, thrusting myself forward with my arms. Then, the doctor at the clinic broke the news to Mom and Dad. Scoliosis, curvature of the spine. It was happening quickly, my spine bending into an S shape, the muscles around it too weak to provide support. The answer, said Dr. Brill, the priest in the white coat, was the Milwaukee back brace, a newly designed medical prosthesis. I remember how cold the word sounded—prosthesis—nothing I would say to a friend.

They fitted me with a steel cage, vertical bars every six inches or so from hip to head, a steel halo round my brow, with a leather chin cup which immobilized my head, a strap across my forehead and a Frankenstein steel tightening screw in the back, with a quarter-sized hex nut protruding. *He'll have to wear this till the spine straightens.* That was the sentence handed down. I returned home, back in the wheelchair. I had to be moved about like a giant vase, placed here and there.

When it was time for Effie to resume her visits, I positioned myself on my bed against the woodwork, steadying myself with the screw head against the wood. When Effie came into the room and saw me, she burst into tears at the sight of the Boy in the Iron Mask, the erector set Humpty Dumpty, the Prisoner of Zenda. She sat on the couch with mom and composed herself before she came back into my room and sat down. I felt her sadness to be greater than mine and couldn't understand why. Perhaps the weight of the world is love.

Every weekday I sat there for a couple of hours up against the wall, listening, learning: Orion, Lepidoptera, Pocahontas, Mohican, Northwest Territory, Eric the Red, John Wilkes Booth, Madagascar, the Andes, Ponce de Leon, Rio De Janeiro, Nagasaki, Hiroshima, Turquoise, Triceratops. The words extended outward in all directions, a bridge to the world. I wrote them down in a big yellow tablet; some were stones, which, when cut and polished, glinted like gems: Dakota, Lizard, Oxen, Pistol. Each word knew what it meant long before I read it.

Finally, after six months of my living in the Milwaukee brace, one night Mom heard me crying. She came into my room. I told her if I had to wear this another year, I'd rather die. I don't know how I mustered the courage to make such a declaration. The next day she and Dad took it off me, straps and bolts, lifted me out of it like a lobster out of a trap. They drove to the Springfield Clinic and gave it back to the doctors who, in turn, informed them, coincidentally, that new data, just released, now indicated that the Milwaukee back brace did little or nothing to correct curvature of the spine. Dr. Brill apologized for any unnecessary suffering that might have been incurred. I was free. I didn't have to die.

This summer, fifty years later, when I returned to the cottage, to the same room where I still sleep when I visit, I traced with my fingertips the woodwork scarred by the steel hex stud on the back of the Milwaukee brace. The scar, a pattern of gouges about the size of my hand, is still visible: a glyph, a character, a tattoo, a sign, an etching, an epigram, a prisoner scratching a count of the days on the cell wall. It marked my hitching post. It kept track of my time in the stocks. It was one of my first attempts to make my mark on the world.

When I graduated from the eighth grade and my home-schooling came to an end, Effie presented me with a gift, a pencil sharpener, a Boston model RS. It is still with me. I have written the rough drafts of these pages with pencils sharpened on it. My fingertips trace these lines, the welt of the words, the gouges in the paper, that woodwork.

Effie did finally marry, a kindly fellow named Bob Ulm, a prosperous local farmer. Dad, mom and I drove out one afternoon to visit her. I was leaving for college in Terre Haute, Indiana. It was early autumn. The farmhouse was surrounded by apple trees, the smell of vinegar in the sugared air, the heavy golden light shafting through the boughs. She was working in the yard. She put down her rake and walked over to the car to greet us. I wanted to tell her of my resolve not to starve dreamlessly, and that, as she stood there, I knew, young as I was, that a Great Wind was carrying us all across the sky. I couldn't find more than a handful of words. A grocery bag of apples handed through the window. A brush of her lips on my cheek. A last wave, and smile, as we turned down the driveway.

She died a year later, cancer. A Great Wind. The Crimes of the World. The Dawn like Thunder. I can still hear Effie in my head, reading me these lines from Tennyson.

And the stately ships go on
to their haven under the hill;
But O for the touch of a vanished hand,
and the sound of a voice that is still.
Break, break, break,
at the foot of thy crags, O sea!
But the tender grace of a day that is dead
Will never come back to me.

A Luminous Phenomenon

There is a spirit, a certain force,
inherent in the blood . . .
and the nature, yea, the soul
in this spirit and blood is identical
with the nature of the stars.
　　　　—William Harvey
　　　　　　Seventeeth Century Physician

I sit down with my doctor,
a young woman in a starched, white coat,
who asks me how I am feeling.
I tell her I cannot jump
as high as I used to,
but I can stay up in the air longer,
that the body is nothing more than
the material aspect of the soul,
and my soul shines like
the full harvest moon
in the cloudless sky.
She reads my brave talk
for what it is: whistling
past the bone yard.
She knows I am waist deep
in muddy water.

My blood pressure.
All my life I have been trying
to get it up, to feed the fire.
Now, she wants it down,
systolic, diastolic, the hard arterial math.
One pill dilates the blood vessels.
Another relaxes the heart muscle,
the *shump shump* thunder pump.
Breath is a wheezing squeeze box.
Narrower is the way,
year by year.

She smiles softly, takes my hands.
We bow our heads in prayer
to our heavenly father
who teaches love is the first wound,
who clears the sugar cane fields
with the blade of his hand,
who gathers the hungry children
unto him that they might taste
the sweetness of his grace.

One night, in 1953,
when I was thirteen, my father
shook me awake and called me out
to the back steps of the cottage on the lake.
It was the summer of the lights,
Aurora Borealis, the northern lights,
great spikes of cold orange fire running
up to the zenith, hot lava cracks in the sky.
My father and I sat, wrapped in a blanket,
watching the lights dance out over the water.

I wanted you to see this,
my father said.
It is caused by a great storm on the sun.

Fishing the Sky Overturned

My Pop and I fished till dark, rowing the small
wooden boat he had built, working the shoreline.
We cast the riprap dam, in close under the shad bushes
where the big chunk largemouth lurked in shadow.
The sky clouded in the west, swallowing the sun.
Light held long on the water. The Great Triangle
of Summer bloomed overhead, anchored by
Deneb in Cygnus; Altair in Aquila; Vega in Lyra.

We rowed home toward the light on the back porch
across the flat black water, the dip of the oars,
the creak of the locks. Pop saw it first, a light
pulsing, tumbling along the northern horizon,
jerking like a fishing lure on the surface of the dark
water overhead. We watched it for a couple
of minutes till it dropped below the tree line.

It was a statellite, Pop confided. I knew the word
was *satellite*, but at fourteen, I didn't correct my Pop.
I just listened and thought about how far away it was.
It belongs to the Russians, the KGB, he whispered.
They are spying on us. I wondered why the KGB
wanted to know about the two of us drifting, unarmed,
in a small wooden boat, on a lake in Illinois.
Statellite. I knew what he meant. That was
good enough. What else can you ask of a word?
Even then, I suspected being right was stony ground.
If I am right, not much is left for you.

Pop drove away from the lake cottage in 1970,
snow birding to Florida where he lived another twenty years.
A neighbor lady found him face down on his kitchen floor.
I burned the warped rowboat, full of dead leaves,
in the back yard, saved the oarlocks, hung on a nail.

It was my Pop's *statellite.* Call it that.
Let it be. His gone star.

The Bird Is Caught Simply by the Leg

Debra Paget. Corrine Calvert. Susan Hayward. Rita Hayworth. Jean Simmons. Diana Dors. Piper Laurie. Jane Russell. Elizabeth Scott. There were dozens more. The stars, the starlets, then fourth or fifth magnitude, hardly visible to my naked eye. Full page faces, studio publicity poses, every imperfection air-brushed away. *Silver Screen* and *Movie Screen* magazines were home to those nineteen fifties sugar plums, most of whom I had met at the Arcadia theater downtown. They couldn't see me, sitting on the back row in the dark. We couldn't see the Hollywood hills from that little farm town of Olney in southeastern Illinois where I was born, but Tinsel Town shipped its dream bundles tossed from the backs of four a.m. delivery trucks, news of the celluloid people, delivered to the Whittle Avenue news stand. Mom made her monthly pilgrimage. Glossies of the beguiling citizens of Tinsel Town. Nobody like that where I'm from.

After Mom had read them a couple of times and tossed them aside, I got this idea. I borrowed one of Dad's single-edged razor blades and began carefully to cut out the photos, lovely women, coiffed, cup caked, ski slope bosoms, eyes to drown in, smiling right at me, an eleven-year-old home schooled kid from Hank Williams Sugardale baloney land. I kept them in a big pile on my bed. Before turning out the lights, I'd leaf through them, like a pubescent Cupid's Tarot deck, sometimes leaning down to kiss the bee-stung lips of that night's beloved, pressing my lips to the page.

Most nights it was Debra Paget. I'd seen her play an Egyptian slave in some dumb Biblical movie at the Arcadia, bare midriff, heaving bosoms, lowered lashes. One night, I wrote, down in the right corner of her photo, *Maj, You are the only one, Debra Paget.* I did it in a fake, feminine cursive, kind of scrolled and loopy. I spent the next couple of hours signing them all. *To Sweet Maj who has stolen my heart, Rita Hayworth. Maj, I cried a river over you, Julie London. Maj, You are the only man in the world for me, Love, Jane Russell. I don't want to live without you, Diana Dors.* I tried to mix up the handwriting so the autographs looked authentic.

The next afternoon, I began thumb tacking all those beautiful faces, with their inscribed pledges of undying love, to the fiberboard walls of my small room, row after row, maybe ten photos across. I covered one wall completely, then another, a third. Maybe a hundred photos edge to edge. Then I lay back on my bed, my small knucklehead on the plumped pillow. All of those breathtaking, hot-eyed women from planet Hollywood held me steadfastly in their attention, untroubled by my skinny shyness, my tongue-tied dreaming. They were the stars. I was a peewee astronomer scanning the night sky.

That following spring, we moved again. I took down the photos, carefully, saved them all in a big manila envelope, my bevy of beauties, Maj's harem of ever smiling loves. I never saw them again. Maybe Mom or Dad packed them off to the burn barrel to free me from that too-early thrall. Maybe they are still in an attic somewhere. My folks might have figured I was too young to give my heart away to Hollywood and its plastic princesses. Maybe they worried I'd not get it back. Maybe I didn't.

Perhaps, the heart is given away only once. Even when you do it, you don't know that's it. Some days now I think my original heart pie got cut up in a hundred or more slices that winter when I was eleven. When I wrote those expressions of love, *Never forget me, Maj. I'll never forget you, Piper Laurie,* that was it. To each I have been faithful, in my own way. Something went out of me that year, an offering, too soon, to something distant and unformed. It did not return. I don't think I would recognize it if it did.

We Contain the Light in Which We Live

All week I have played Scrabble
with my eleven-year-old grandson Liam Michael.
After supper, we spread out the board,
dump the wooden letters and laugh and talk the game
to one another. We learned strange
new words this week: the Z words.

Zebu—an Asiatic ox

Ziggurat—a Mesopotamian tower, a
temple, a lofty pyramidal structure
built in successive stages with
outside staircases and a shrine at
the top.

Ziram—an organic zinc used as a
rubber acculator
and an agricultural fungicide.

Try *Zoea*—an early larval form of
decapod crustaceans.

Or *Zoysia*—a genus of creeping
perennial grasses.

It goes on—the ten-point
Z letter words—and the eight-point
X—really is something other than
the fourteenth letter of the Greek alphabet. It
is also an unstable particle of the
baryon family existing in both negative
and neutral change states.

And *Quipu*—the ten-point Q letter,
a device for calculation made by varicolored
cords attached and knotted and used by the
Ancient Peruvians.

The strange, lovely new words
tumble against one another in my head
like little wooden carnival boats
as Liam nods off to sleep
on the couch beside me.

Words, how they join us
in intricate imaginings in a shared world.
Gather words as if they were food.
Arrange them in your head, on the page.
Someday you will be called forth
to defend your own truth.

Liam Michael,
you will need your own words,
the ones that come to you in the night,
the ones you speak
to the children, to the dying,
to a loved one who has turned
to the long walk away.
They will not begin with Z or Q or X.

The words may be easier to spell
and harder to understand:
Food, Love, Forgive.
You name the others.
Trust that we will know
what you mean.

Halim El Dabh, His 90th Birthday

Each of us has many names.
The gods are within us and without us.
Halim El Dabh, one of his other names
is Shango, after the Yoruba God of thunder and lightning,
The God of drums, the God of dance.
Thunder is lightning crying out.
Lightning is the birth crown of thunder.

This week, in the first hours of March,
the month of Halim's birth,
the month of our renewal,
a line of midnight thunderstorms drummed
its way through Kent, thunderstorms,
the quarrel of light and darkness,
of heaven and earth.
It was the big drum of Shango we heard.
The big drum of Halim,
calling forth the music of thunder,
shaking us from our sleep, calling us to the dance.
Halim, restless as always at midnight,
drumming on the taut goat hide,
drumming on the one heart we share.

In mid life, Halim was struck by
a lightning bolt thrown from the heavens
to remind him that he is forever
a child of lightning, a child of thunder,
marked by lightning, blessed by lightning,
filled with a light that has not diminished.

It has been an honor for those of us
lucky enough to travel this road with him.
Let there be light.
Let there be lightning.
Let the drums speak in their voices
of thunder.

The Dancer Moves Toward the Light

for Brandon after his improvisation

The first man emerges from the cave
of night.
His eyes are closed.

He awakes on his side,
knees against his chest.
A hand flutters like a bird
at the end of its tether.
A foot begins to tremble,
longing to begin the journey,
quivering to walk away.

He rises to his feet,
against the earth pull.

His body is strange to him
as he feels his own flesh
for the first time.

He stands like a crossbow,
his arms extended,
the bolt of his body
aimed toward Heaven.

He steadies himself
like a man in a rocking boat
on a great sea of dream.

A moment of ease, on one knee,
as he fills with the spirit
God has breathed into him.

His eyes open.

Pharmacy

Al Bartle, the old Nashville drummer now off the road forever, is set up by the Portage County Housing Authority in a low-income apartment in downtown Ravenna, Ohio. He stares down at empty storefronts and the flickering year-round Christmas lights strung across the Buckeye Bar. A health aide shows up twice a day to tend to his needs, to microwave lunch and tidy up. A caseworker brings Al his weekly groceries and sorts out his meds in a plastic day planner.

Not much ahead, but down below is the Triangle Pharmacy where Al wanders the aisles daily, searching for anything cheap to buy on his forty bucks a month allowance. Every purchase, nail clippers, pipe cleaners, a Milky Way bar, is an excuse to talk to the woman at the cash register. All Al has ever wanted to do is talk with women, to think about them, to be around them, to taste their breath. Last week, he told me that the lovely Miss Somebody and he brushed forearms as they were reaching across the Band Aid display. Al said it was like sticking his thumb in an electric socket, just that butterfly touch, about more than he can stand.

At 7:00 a.m. last Thursday morning, the cardio doctors at the Cleveland Clinic rolled Al out of bed and told him to lie down under the knife. Ten years ago the docs in Akron had cracked him open and replaced a heart valve with one from a pig. Al oinked his way through the whole decade, drinking, smoking, relishing the carnal life, front-row man at the tittie bar. Then one day, he couldn't breathe. Dead piggy valve. No more oinks. This time, they cut him open and plugged in a cow valve. I told him, before they turned out the lights, "See you round the pasture when you wake up, old friend." "Yep," says Al, "Moo . . . Moo."

He remains an undiscovered moon of tenderness in thrall to an Earth on which he woke seventy-four years ago. A waning moon rising late in the east now, held by the bare trees, its soft light touching the sleeping houses.

The Lame Goat Makes His Way to the High Country

Summer solstice,
I am lying belly down
on the hard ground,
not a breath of air,
the spent gods at repose.
The string of prayer flags
across the backyard, spring's
dirty laundry, hangs still,
panels of blue, white, red, green,
yellow, the Bodhisattva Tara tattooed
on each by Heaven's hand.

The Bleeding Heart bush against the fence
has pushed above the Lady of Guadalupe,
Sorrowful Mother of mine hidden
in the tumble of the new green.
My heart is not hidden from her.

I bow my head and pray
that she come to me and place
her soft hands on my gray head.
It is not words I want from her,
but her touch. Let her cool fingers
burn my cheekbones, brand me
as her own wandering child.
So that when the time comes
she might find me among the others
and gather me home.

Somewhere far below me,
the earth creaks a turn on the iron pole.

Willows

Blessed are Those Who Mourn
—Norman O. Brown

It was the mid nineteen forties.
The war was on the other side
of the ocean. I was five years old.
No school yet; I couldn't read or write.
My grandparents' farm was my home that summer.
I wandered the fencerows,
the boundaries at the wood's edge.
Even then the puzzle was forming:
why everyone I knew was hiding
something, coloring in the empty spaces
the way I did with my crayons.

One summer noon, my Grandma Blanche
packed a picnic basket. We found shade
beneath the willows along the branch
meandering through the pasture.
I played in the green tresses hanging
into the ankle-deep water sparkling its way
over sand and pebbles.
The half dozen willows leaned against
one another, whispering in the heat,
old women still green from their tears.

Grandma called them *weeping willows.*
I heard her say *weeping widows.*

No, she smiled, *It's willows.*

Now, after all these years, count sixty,
I am certain it is *widows, weeping.*

Jolly Roger

One summer Sunday, a young woman entered her church, found her pew, stood and opened her hymnal. She was about ten rows back from the pulpit, toward the middle. The congregation, led by the minister, was well into "Leaning on the Everlasting Arms" when she caught his evangelical eye. She was bare from the waist up. He locked his arms at the elbows, gripped the pulpit, drew himself up and proclaimed. *My good woman, you cannot enter the house of God naked. This is holy ground.* The woman did not blink, nor cover her bosom. She retorted. *I am a member of this congregation. I take communion from your hand at this rail. I am absolved of sin. I am free. I do this because I have a divine right.* Said the preacher, who could do no other than tell the plain truth, *Sister, not only do you have a divine right, you also have a luscious left, but you cannot come into my church naked.*

A big-bellied truck driver told this story one aimless winter afternoon at the Jolly Roger donut shop, just up Route 8 from the Northfield race track where I have tithed over the years. A handful of us straddled red vinyl stools. A thin country woman, jet black Tammy Wynette coif and bangled wrists, worked the thirsty counter and hosted the refugees. She threw back her head and cackled, accepting the homely gift, finding nothing to offend. Everyone there found shelter in the story, in the laughter, as we sat in the belly of that beached and windowed whale, the Jolly Roger.

In the hills to the north, a homeless young man sat hugging himself, rocking on his heels, dreaming of sugar glaze, hot coffee, safe sleep between a woman's breasts. Night was coming. The small fire had flickered out.

Kamikaze, That Divine Wind

My mother is dissolving like an Alka-Seltzer
in the warm waters of this Indian Summer,
the white crown of her head
unraveling hair by hair,
flung outward toward the Crab nebula, the fiery
burrow from which we came.

The carbon in these chains that
bind flesh to spirit was
born in that hot galactic heart
that could no longer contain itself.
The big fizz is still expanding.

My mother's life is now a small bang, a hushed
dissolution, what the white coats have named
anxiety attacks, her little apartment abuzz
with swarms of tiny Kamikaze planes, the pilots
drunk on sake and crazed devotion, diving at
her little boat paddling the burning oil slick.
I can't see them. She can. I know they are there.

The glass jar shatters on the sidewalk.
The fire flies mill about, then gather toward home.

A Hungry Ghost Surrenders His Tackle Box

My friend Bill Hupp leaves this week,
a year's stay, Zen Mountain monastery,
nestled in the Catskills.
He must surrender his things before
he can give himself away, cut his ties
to the world, gray house on Longcoy Street,
green Ford Taurus, bachelor's kit and kaboodle.
He must now trust the sangha,
the community with whom he will train
to live the Four Noble Truths,
to dig through the compost heap
of his suffering and cart it away.

This rainy March afternoon
Bill lays down his burdens at my house.
I am to find solace in attachment
to what he must renounce.
A two-foot stack of *Tricycle,*
the Buddhist review, thousands of bent
word keys to the Pure Land, how to shoe
the Wind Horse, how to jumpstart
the dharma in your neighborhood.

He hands me a sheaf of his own
pissed off, gotta bless you anyway poems,
fuel for his heart's fire.
He drags in a rolled up, inflatable
rubber raft, a ten footer, heavy duty,
Lake Erie tested, with red plastic oars
and a handy foot pump: three hundred steps
should do it. And Bill gives me his tackle box.
I have never heard of a man
surrendering his tackle box,
short of the death bed.

Fishing is an attachment which he must sever.
Otherwise, he'll remain a hungry ghost
hiding a can of worms, sneaking out of sesshin
to fish the monastery pond.
I accept his gift because I must,
a big, multiple drawer Plano stuffed
with plastic worms, crusty jars of pork rinds,
jointed minnows, silver buck tail spoons.
I open it once, then consign it to the basement.
Belongings, the little one word book of law.
We cannot belong to our longings.
We must be our longings.
I don't know another path.

Bill, don't forget to come back
for what you can't belong to,
rubber raft, tackle box, words,
the rest of this stuff
which, as the Buddhists teach,
are phenomena that rise and set
only in the mind.

V

Never forget you begin somewhere
in the mountains, far to the north
where snow and sky join.

First Call for Poets

If you want to be happy for a day, get drunk. For a week, kill a pig. For a month, get married. For life, be a gardener. So goes the Chinese proverb. I haven't had a drink in over seven years. That's off the table, no more hiding out in the barn with John Barleycorn. I did once witness a pig being butchered at my grandparents' farm. I can still hear the squeal as old man Pinky Beavers straddled the pig and stuck a butcher knife in his ear. That didn't make me happy. Not me or Pinky or the pig. I am married and gladly so. The months grow into years. I am not exactly a gardener, but I did plant some begonias and impatiens off the back porch. That did feel good, digging in the rich, dark soil, firming the roots, watching the bloom rear and spread.

I stumbled across another quote in my journal, this time from an anonymous Thai forest monk: *Oh, what joy to discover there is no happiness to be found in this world.* The very notion of happiness has always puzzled me. From childhood, it was out there, as a goal, as an ideal state of being, and it was always tied to love. Then, this one: someone or something making you happy. Muddy waters from there on out. Joy is not ramped-up happiness. Happiness is a fig tree. Joy is a mountain.

The ancient Greeks believed that the highest happiness might be that moment when we see things plainly, even the terrible, for what they are, grounded in the truth, that inescapable recognition. They called it *Anagnorisis.* It has little to do with feeling good, secure, complete, fulfilled. There is nothing beyond this knowing, except perhaps a cleansing joy. If you do ever come across that proverbial drunken, pig killing, married gardener, ask him if he is happy. Make him tell you the truth. If you bump into Oedipus on the trail, where the three roads meet, he who found the awful truth about himself, ask him about *Anagnorisis.* Do not flinch at his answer. That forest monk, the joyful one, you are not likely to find. You may hear his laughter at the edge of the woods.

Soon the first frost, then winter. These poetry readings are a gaggle of word pilgrims gathered around such fire as we can bring. Heraclitus believed that our lives are an exchange of fire—fire unto fire in the dark labyrinth. The good poet Wendell Berry reminds us that the universe is almost totally dark. Little islands of light dot the great emptiness. A cluster of poems shines forth tonight. An exchange of fire unto fire, poem unto poem. Warmth, light, the Friday night poetry reading is open. Hold high your torch.

The Garden Entrusted to Us

for Lisa Coffman

I am on my annual westward pilgrimage, a five hundred-mile road trip, back to where I was raised, a small lake cottage north of Olney, Illinois. Last night, half way, I laid over in Celina, Ohio, hard up against the Indiana border. The headwaters of the mighty Wabash River begin twenty miles west of here, a creek you could leap across. There is much to love in headwaters, clarity gathering itself fresh before pushing toward the muddy heart of the world. The map of every life. I am on the shore of an inland sea, uncounted acres of corn and soybean fields, newly planted. The distances rear up, then rush away from me. I find an old and abiding comfort in farm country. Fixing one's attention on a horizon centers the emotional life, like the bubble in the carpenter's level steadying in its measure. Tomorrow, I am going home. I feel that old pull at my breastbone.

The first night back in Illinois, we row the old jon boat down to the dam, Vernor Lake, where the Fox Creek watershed was dammed in 1898 by men, shovels and horse drawn wagons. Every year, late May has been the height of the honeysuckle bloom, the entire earthen dam festooned in white and pale-yellow blossoms. What we find this spring is one long wound, an eighth of a mile, scabbed with dead brown foliage. The city maintenance crew has been here with Roundup weed killer spray. We drift a while, staring at the ruins. The witch has eaten the children, again. For decades, we have lingered here, stoned on the fragrance that rode the evening breeze up from the river bottoms, circling, beguiling. One year, as we glided along the dam, a young woman literally rose up out of the honeysuckle, a languid lift to her feet. She was blonde and white, like the blossoms out of which she rose. She began to walk away from us, carrying her fishing rods, toward the veiled entrance back to her world. Gone. A friend later chuckled and told me her name is Mickey, that she lives in the nearby trailer court. Not what I saw. I caught a glimpse of a shimmering gown, a galaxy of goldfinches crowning her head. I felt something turn in my chest.

These lines of Machado come back to haunt me.

What have you done with the Garden
That was entrusted to you?

Her garden is destroyed. She won't be back in my lifetime. What they were entrusted with they have violated. There is no cure for the hatred of beauty. Perhaps they have already wrecked the gardens inside themselves and cannot bear to witness the outward sign of what they have destroyed. Perhaps they have been caught by what Boehme called *the spirit of the outward world.* You and I, let us abide and turn that spirit away from everything we love. Let us tend to every bloom, without, within, that has been entrusted to us.

Fishing with Jim O'Neill

for Sean Kelly Ragain

Everything has its story folded into it. Most stories are lost or never get told. Let's save this one. These fishing lures I send you belonged to an old fisherman named Jim O'Neill whose lifeboat sank this past year. His daughter came down the driveway at the garage sale last Sunday to hand me the boxes of lures as I sat in the car. *I'll take $4.50 for everything,* she said. *They belonged to my father Jim O'Neill. He came down with cancer; then four months later a heart attack took him. He loved to fish. We sold off everything this morning except these lures.* She smiled and waved goodbye. *Thank you.* A clean slate. It is all gone, detritus, leftovers, treasures, things of the heart with which we touch the world. We don't get to keep anything. Even our names will finally be lost.

These flash and funk lures, half-a-foot long, with day-glow spangles, whirligig willow-blades, fluorescent hula skirts and buzz-bomb rosary beads. I got no idea what kind of fish they lure. Marlin? Bluefin Tuna? King Salmon? Sailfish? They look more like Christmas tree ornaments or a doodad a Gangbanger might wear round his neck or souvenirs thrown from a Mardi Gras float. This isn't art imitating nature. Nothing like this swims in any waters we know.

This is about Jim O'Neill, whose name I want you to remember when you troll or cast one of his lures. They are brand new. He never got a chance to fish them. Do it for him. Hang one on a Weeping Willow tree to show the world Jim O'Neill died for love. Dangle one from the G-string of red-hot Hannah the pole dancer in gratitude that the heart is forever unmapped territory. Hand one to some peewee fisher-boy with his old Zebco outfit, casting by a stone bridge you will have to cross one midnight, alone. Offer a pair to that Tlingit Indian princess you met on the Northwest Passage, one for each pierced ear. Fashion a necklace round Miss Boettler as she keeps her solitary granite watch in Kent's Standing Rock Cemetery. Clip one to your belt loop as you step up to the craps table on your next swing through Vegas. Drop one into the offering plate at church when it is passed down your row.

Stand up in your boat, cut the line and throw one as far as you can, out into the deep where all things return. This is for you, Sean. This is for Jim O'Neill. Make a place for him in the small boat we share, heading for that far shore.

The Mark of My Father's Hand

for Ted Lyons

It is a fine summer day here at the lake house in Olney, north breeze, crackling blue skies, one of those days where you are glad to be in it, no tombstones in the head or muck in the blood. My son Sean and the neighbor Bradley are tearing off the old siding on the cottage and replacing it with plywood. We have owned this place since 1952. Each layer peeled away reveals the mark of my father's hand. He was a carpenter by trade. Dad salvaged leftover materials from job sites and used them on our little house. In these boards we are finding today, covered by siding and tar paper for fifty years, the salvaged nails Dad drove are neatly spaced, each head perfectly flat. I can still hear Dad's hammer, three strikes, then done, always three. If he bent a nail, I never saw it. He passed on in 1990. I hear his grandson nailing the new wood on the other side of the house, his strong arm, three beats to the bar. Presence. I believe that when people go away, it is as if they step around the corner of a house, as if into another dimension, very close to us. We just can't see them. As you read this, you are aware of my presence though you can't see me.

The heat has returned, big, stupefying, hot brimstone breath from the plains. One hundred eight degrees here a few days ago, still above 100 degrees each day, another week of it promised. The lake is freckled with islands of floating moss you can damn near walk across. It is as warm as spit. No swimming or fishing. Local word is the entire corn crop has been cooked, no rain in months here in the five counties that comprise southeastern Illinois. The soybeans will soon be a total loss also. This is farm country, the ancient cycle, seeds in the ground, the annual gamble against the gods we now name El Nino, La Nina, who rule the ocean currents and the sky. The roll of the dice came up snake eyes this year.

Most days I open all the notebooks, poems and scatter them around me, here on the front porch where I set up camp, just as I do on the floor in the living room. I've never had an office at home, never wanted one. I choose to wash my dirty clothes midstream, the feel of everything flowing around me, tugging at me. Decades ago, a sentence stuck with me, *Use the days you have left to deepen your life.* So I have quietly become a digger, working to widen and bring more depth to this life, this ongoing imagining. You tell me, *Be alert. And be kind.* I do recognize the truth of that, how it serves, and I try to move that thought to the forefront, to be guided by it. Otherwise, I just wander from thing to thing, caught by shine and jingle. We tell each other our stories, and at the core of every story is something nameless and beyond the reach of language. The awareness that it is there, though hidden, is enough for me to live on. It has to be enough.

Soon, the humming heat will find me here on the porch. The shade of the Oaks will retreat. I may sleep away this afternoon. The cicada have begun their late-summer songs in the woods across the road. I long to learn their language and forget my own.

Fold Your Dirty Clothes/Build a Paper Boat

for Liam Michael Ragain

You told me you wanted to learn about Zen Buddhism. I am sending you *Taking the Path of Zen* by Roshi Robert Aitken. A place to begin. A place to end. My beat up copy I bought at Naropa Institute for Buddhist Studies, Boulder, Colorado, in 1983, where I spent a week at a conference on Eastern and Western contemplative traditions. Trappist monks, Benedictine Monks, Greek Orthodox priests, Carmelite nuns, Zen Buddhists, Tibetan Buddhists. That was the real Super Bowl for me. The weeklong topic was *Compassion*, how we can open that inside ourselves and then act out of that in our daily lives. The leader was the Tibetan teacher Chogyam Trungpa, the founder of Naropa. He didn't say anything all week. He just sat, listened with a fixed, bemused smile. On the last day, after everyone had chewed the topic to tatters, a young woman turned to him and asked, *Master, What is compassion?*

He paused and, in a soft voice, said this. *Compassion is washing your clothes and drying your clothes and folding your clothes.* A murmur of confoundment rippled through the gathering. I think I get it, at least part of it. Compassion is something we do. Compassion without action doesn't mean much. So, I went back to the spare bedroom where I was staying with a Buddhist friend. I washed the sheets, the covers, the towels, whatever I had used, dried them and folded them neatly. I did it gratefully, with mindfulness, not daydreaming, but with attention not to myself but to the task. I still fold my clothes each night before I go to bed, even if they are dirty, in gratitude for how they have served me, sheltered me, kept me warm. So, we make little camps of order surrounded by deep darkness. We build our little paper boats and launch them into mountainous seas. It is the little things we do that hold the big world together, for one another.

The gathering that final day was held in a big stone church in downtown Boulder. All the dignitaries were lined up on the stage. Each spoke, a summing up, a final imprint. Most memorable for me was Sister Tessa Bielicki, a Carmelite nun, mid thirties, beautiful beyond all effacement, an ample shining. Fifty feet away, she warmed my cheek-bones. She offered this, which I wrote down, as she spoke, on the inside cover of *Taking the Path of Zen.*

Ten Guidelines for the Path of Christian Contemplation

1. *Work with the Plain Stuff of Day to Day.*
2. *Love God. The Historical Christ from the Scriptures, the Cosmic Christ from Nature, the Mystical Christ from Prayer.*
3. *Love Life & Be Grateful*
4. *Embrace Little Deaths and Little Sufferings for They Prepare Us for the Greater Ones to Come.*
5. *Love One Another & Express it Generously.*
6. *Keep Your Balance.*
7. *Work with Your Humanness.*
8. *Get Back Up Quickly.*
9. *Sit Still. Empty Yourself Every Day. Be Still.*
10. *Laugh No Matter What Happens, Especially at Yourself.*

More than thirty years later, I still turn to these guidelines. And I still remember sitting on the church steps that evening when Sister Bielicki brushed past me. I hailed her. She came back up the steps. I offered her my thanks and my hand. When we clasped, Liam, it felt as if I had gripped flame, the fire of the life deep within her. Not just her life moving within her, but the greater life that finds expression in each of us, the life forged in the fiery mind of God.

If I, if you, can keep even a couple of these truths in the forefront each day, they become points of light by which we navigate and find our way home. Use what you can. *Love Life & Be Grateful.* If you do that, it would be a victory for us all.

Everything falls under the law of change, like a dream, a phantom, a bubble, a shadow, like dew or a flash of lightning; you should contemplate like this.
     —Diamond Sutra

Everything falls under the law of change. Never forget that. Everything. Learn to live in accord with that. So many stories I want to share with you, so little time. I want to know your life, the real life, how it really is for you. I want you to know my life. That is what this letter is all about. Another beginning. And about the path we're on together. The trail is narrowing for me. I will be seventy-four in a couple of days. I'll stay with you as long as I can. Our lives are *like dew or a flash of lightning.*

I leave you with a little poem one of the veterans I work with gave me. Learn it by heart. When you are confronted by Big Stupidity with its loud, metallic voice, when your truth is threatened, when anyone threatens to diminish you or shame you, stand up and bark this at them. Make them eat this bread.

> *Life is mostly froth and bubble*
> *these two things stand like stone*
> *kindness for another's trouble*
> *courage in our own.*

Kindness and courage, Liam, my grandson. You will not need much else. Let's find each other before the winter off Lake Erie shuts us down. And remember, the stars always shine, even at noon.

A Page from This Day

I ask the towhead boy
fishing below the Rock Creek waterfall,
the deep pool, *Have you caught anything?*
Naw, an hour ago people were swimming here.
Up the creek, a deputy dawg pulls off
a dozen pistol rounds, crack, crack, crack.
The cane-pole boy hooks a big sunfish
and holds it up to me, grinning, a solar kite
filling the sky.

Later that day, I watch old man Jerry
drag himself into Ciccone's bar,
wash-rag arm, scuffle shoe.
He hangs his stroke cane and climbs his stool.
Roberta has already poured his beer,
caught in the June afternoon yellow fin light
streaming through the open door.

Jerry slumps over his beer.
Under his hat, he is swimming buck naked
in a spring-fed river with a woman
who splashes away, laughing, otter quick.

The Brief Life of Honeysuckle

That evening in Illinois
on Vernor Lake down by the dam,
we were fishing the last light.
The spring sky had cleared
after an hour of hard rain.

For a week, the wild honeysuckle
had been in full bloom, a quarter-
mile spangle along the dam, gold and white blossoms,
the sweet musky scent lifting us
out of the boat, out of our hard shells.

The sunset kissed clouds had turned
a pale ostrich pink, before fading.
Then, a burst of sound. I looked up
just as they flashed overhead,
a great horned owl pursued by one
red-winged blackbird, colors flared,
and led by another red-wing.

A few seconds, and they wheeled around
a stand of trees. Gone. Sixteen-year-old
on the way back to the dock,
came back to me: *God has made a polish
for everything that tarnishes.
And the polish for the heart is remembrance.*

What brushed past me this evening?
That dark wing polishes my heart,
even now.

Groundhog Day Meditation

This morning the delivery man pitched
the daily *Akron Beacon Journal*
down at the sidewalk's end, again.
No news for me today.
My wife has left next to the coffee pot
a brown paper bag wadded inside
a big zip lock baggie.
I am hungry but afraid to open it.

Some days I am spooked
by the inside of everything.
I know she loves me, but
I don't know what I expect:
a handful of candy hearts,
a saint's ear, a fresh scalp,
a drowned man's bible.
After an hour and two cups of coffee,
I unzip the double seal baggie
and slowly crinkle open the brown bag.
Two biscotti, one half eaten,
a half-moon teeth mark.
That's the one I want.

I don't remember closing the bathroom door.
Suppose I turn the knob
and find Chewbaca sitting on the can,
reading yesterday's sports page,
and he turns and grunts to me,
in that garbled voice,
Leave me alone.

I am never alone.
A daddy pops groundhog,
as big as a third grader, has set up
camp under the front porch.
We've lived with him all summer.
He has turned our garden into his root cellar,

his salad bar, standing on his hind legs to nip
at the garnish of flowers.

Three times, I've called the official Kent City
animal trapper. He shows up in
his truck, unloads the Havahart
trap, baits it with a slice of apple and peanut butter.
Mr. Whistle Pig can't resist, though he
knows better. We all know better.
Bang goes the door behind him.
I ask the animal control guy,
What do you do with these groundhogs after you catch 'em?
I take 'em to my boss's farm in Macedonia.

My hunch is he drives three blocks,
hangs a right into Standing Rock cemetery,
turns loose his co-worker
with a slap on his furry butt.
See you next week.
Get along home now.

I cannot bring myself to kill him,
this harmless herbivore,
something about how he scurries away,
wiggling his little behind, an easy mark
for any predator. I am no predator,
though I have eaten three hamburgers
and the breast of a chicken this week.
I pay someone else to do my killing.
But, yesterday, my wife LuAnn came in
with the morning mail, banging
the storm door behind her.

Guess what
that groundhog did . . . he ate the jack o
lantern that little Camille Smith
carved . . . he just ate it . . . all that's
left are pieces scattered on the sidewalk.

Ten-year-old Camille sat here on
the living room floor, old newspapers
spread around her and spent an hour carving
a pumpkin into a friendly ghost,
big slashed welcoming smile, a tiny
triangle nose, big lopsided eyes.
We even added ears, little half-moons,
before we lit the candle amidst a
smattering of applause. Oh, shine
on, brave little goblin, through the long night.
A child's talisman against whatever lurks in the darkness.
The groundhog must have lifted his skullcap
and eaten him for breakfast.

This is no holy war . . . no jihad.
It is entirely secular but he is no longer welcome.
Some accord has been broken,
an unspoken treaty violated.
Start with the traditional solutions,
wheelbarrows of dirty, urine soaked
cat litter down into his burrow,
then rags soaked with ammonia and bleach
poked down the hole with a long
pole, then roman candles and various
other incendiary devices launched down
the tunnel, maybe a dead man's shoe,
stuffed with a crow carcass,
every mojo in the black book.

If that fails, I'll paint my face
orange with a big goofy smile,
hide behind the rhododendron bush
and wait for him as he emerges from his den.
He'll creep toward me,
his breakfast belly growling. I'll hold
steady my jack-o'- lantern head. Closer.
We'll stare deep into each other's eyes.
I'll know his heart. He'll know mine.
Gotcha. I'll bag him, toss him into the trunk

of my 1999 Geo touring sedan and make
that five-hour drive down to Cincinnati,
cross the bridge to Newport, Kentucky,
turn him loose in the first fast food parking lot.
He won't swim the Ohio river
or cross the bridge, even at midnight.
Farewell, little fat brother,
little dumpster diver, buck-toothed murderer
of a child's Halloween dream, wrecker
of the lighthouse of hope. If you can
find your way back to Kent, I'll move out.
The house is yours. Move the family in. I quit.

The coffee is gone. No more biscotti.
Chewbacca just flushed the toilet.
I hear him washing his hands.
He'll be out in a minute.

We do live in a dream world, of strings and
things, light and shadow joining.
Beyond the blue sky, it is so cold.

I turn to today's message in the
Daily Word, the inspirational guide,
a gift subscription from my mother.
She requests large print for me now.
This day's lesson is from Matthew 6:26:

Look at the birds of the air.
They neither sow nor reap nor
gather into barns, and yet your
heavenly Father feeds them. Are
you not of more value than they?

I don't know that my life is of more
value than that of the furry, hungry brother
who lives under the front porch.
I sow. He reaps. He gathers.

Every day is another groundhog day.
I am learning to live with my leaden shadow.

At the Poker Table, at Sea

the dharma is not a flower one can smell

Tonight, we sit down to play poker
at a table strewn with money and gunny sacks
of low-tide mussels, leavened
by the good salty antler talk
of free men dancing in the gun sights.
All games tread dark water.
Everyone here is willing to drown.

Wild Bill hides the queen of hearts in his whiskers.
Theo lowers himself into the pit
where all wrong cards crawl off to die.
Mick the lawyer practices gambling
as the mean little brother of jurisprudence.
Jon shakes his snow globe of quarters,
chanting juju, mojo, low hole card wild.
No faces on my cards; the house is never full.

I have set up my pup tent in the landfill.
I don't do much to resist what is coming, these days.

Outside, a midnight storm sweeps over us,
bending the trees, washing rain
over the roof of the house.
I fold my hand, cash in, close my eyes
and begin to dream we are wallowing
the heavy seas across the Adriatic toward Corfu,
where I found myself twenty years ago,
just off the western Greek coast.

When the skies clear at dawn,
we will step out onto the deck.
The young women of the town
will gather at the dock
to greet our return,
waving, smiling, holding up to us
our children we've never seen,
searching among us for one honest face.

Lament for Stella Gibson

The seventies in southeastern Illinois
were recession times. The oil fields had dried up.
The Roadmaster bicycle factory had broken
the union, gone bottom dollar.
The Walmart cathedral of tomorrow was on the drawing board,
its gridded parking acres still soybeans.
Lots of folks in Olney, my hometown, signed up down
on Boone street, the unemployment office.
The only work I could find was at the local
radio station, two dollars an hour,
news man, music man, trash man, third-class
radio engineer, on the air from six till eleven every night.
Just me and the three blinking red lights on the tower.

The music play list was soft contemporary
middle of the road bonehead oatmeal for the ear.
Sundown come and the phone would begin to ring.
Requests, complaints, questions, rants, offers of love.

Calls from pissed off, hormone humped
teenagers who demanded Black Sabbath heavy metal or else,
from warehouse fork lift truck drivers craving Elvis,
from Joe Smith, the coin collecting barber who
never told me the same gorilla joke twice,
from a waitress at the Red Rooster truck stop
who couldn't make it through the night
without a Kenny Rogers love song.
I'd hear from half-in-the-bag housewives
who wanted their hearts jumpstarted by Barry Manilow.

Every night I'd get a phone call or two
from Stella, Stella Gibson.
Hello, this is WVLN WSEI fm.
Hello, honey, I couldn't live without you
playing this music, keeping me company,
talking to me in the dark.

Stella was in her late seventies,
long time blind, living alone
in a poor neighborhood dubbed Goosenibble,
down by the Baltimore and Ohio tracks.
One night after the sign-off news,
and I'd shut down the transmitter,
the phone rang. It was Stella again.
Honey, I am lonesome tonight.
I sure wish I had me a cold beer
and some company.
What kind of beer you like, Stella?
I like them tall boys, nice and cold.

An hour later, I knocked on her screen door.
Stella appeared, flowered housecoat,
hair tied back with a scarf, small shoulders.
I want to see what you look like, she said
and took my face in her hands,
thumbs along cheekbones and brow,
down the nose, lips, chin, dimple.
When she had me in her head,
she led me to her kitchen table.

We split the six pack
as she told me stories about her cats,
her dead husbands, her no good hillbilly neighbors,
her rag rug business.
She made jumble-colored rag rugs
and sold them on the radio station's call in
morning show *Quiz n' Tell.*
After her third beer, she loaded me down
with five rugs and kissed me a midnight goodbye,
a quick, squeegee smack at the side of the mouth.
Honey, she said, *Don't you be expecting*

to come around here every night.
One foot out the door, an armful of rugs,
I turned back to her.
Your name Stella, it means star.

I never saw her again,
though a couple of times, I did leave
a six pack of Pabst blue ribbon on her doorstep.
I quit the ghost voice business
that November, packed my Impala
oil burner and wandered east,
following rivers, sleeping in truck stop lots.

A few years later, a hometown fella
told me Stella Gibson had passed on.
You know she didn't make those rugs.
They come from Guatemala.
She had them shipped down from Chicago.
I know that guy. He doesn't believe in much.

She is in her dark kitchen tonight,
sipping the foam of a tall boy.
Singing along with the radio.
Her sure fingers weave the thin rag strips,
pulling the colors through.

I was the night man.
She was a star.

I Will Tell You a Mystery

Across the street, here in Provincetown,
the gray, shingled house is silent,
nestled in the heavy August morning.
The curtains are drawn,
windows cantilevered outwards.

A burst of words, steel jacketed
and spittled, as the old man yells
at his wife, *expect the unexpected.*
then, long quiet.

Midafternoon, he shouts at her again,
No more candy. No more candy.

The house sinks like a stone
into evening.

Sugar turns to salt.

One cannot touch without being touched.

Sleeping in Provincetown

All flesh is grass
—Book of Isaiah

I feel my wife's hand on my bare back,
a slow, gentle circling, lightly touching,
shoulder blade to hip, fingers walking the crooked
cobblestone of spine, reading the braille of skin.
It rouses me from the shallow ditch of sleep.
The red-eyed numbers 3:00 a.m. watch from the bedside table.

She is dreaming, finger painting the empty canvas
of my back, as she did the black spikes of the harbor's broken pier
pilings, against the molten lava of yesterday's sun
drowning in the cold Atlantic.

She is cleaning the storm window the seasons have set
between us, the years of palm prints pressed to the glass,
the life lines, the heart lines, that flow together, split and rejoin.

She is working the bellows of my breath,
the latticed stretch of ribs, skinny accordion man,
calling forth a music I have not learned to play,
a music only she and I will hear.

She is listening with her fingertips
for the faintest tapping from the miners
in the coal shafts of my belly
buried beyond rescue, their last whispers
to one another echoing off an anthracite sky.

A Ouija board cursor glides over my back,
guided not by her hand, but by another,
the hand that guides the swallowtail in her resolute drift
from flower to flower, that guides the dying man,
having surrendered his clothes and shoes, toward the dim outline
of a door frame he remembers from childhood.

She is dowsing for my heart,
her peach twig fingers arcing
to that wellspring from which we both long to drink,
that living water I can taste only from her mouth.

Counting the Stitches

for John Reeves

John Reeves and I were down the third base side of home plate at the Akron Aeros game last night. It went to the bottom of the 15th, just short of midnight, when the Aeros' first baseman Jesus Aguilar bounced one through a drawn-in infield. Big jubilation, that jump and pile-on thing the players must have learned from televised games. By then, there were about as many on the field and dugouts as in the stands. The moment we came for, the one to keep alive up under your ribs, was the pitch just before the winning hit.

A foul ball. I told John, *It's comin' back to you.* The ball bounced off the concrete below us, twenty feet or so straight back, a smaller hop, another on the step. It rolled right up to John's feet. I have known him thirty years. It was a look I've never seen before. Tongue tied jubilation or something deeper blooming, perhaps what Ivan Illich writes about, how, in the most unlikely of circumstances you may come to a point of grace, in which a voice not your own, says, *You are accepted.* Just that. Accepted by and in the universe. Everywhere is suddenly home. You can finally forget about chasing love in all its Halloween disguises. You are accepted. Did John hear that voice? *After fifty years of baseball games, this is my first ball,* said John. Turning it over and around, thumbing the stitches. If it isn't yours, you can't have it.

When the stadium lights do go out for John, may he remember how that foul ball found him unerringly that late May night in Akron, how it completed what had begun so long ago.

I have been listening for that voice since my early teens when I first began to awaken to my little life and the greater, ongoing life of which it is, briefly, a part. I remember one November evening I rolled to the side of the house, the cottage on the Illinois lake where I was raised. I turned into a sharp, chilling north wind across the water. The leaves were down; the light was dying. I sat there, closed my eyes and felt the cold find me up under my jacket. I burst into tears. One big sob. Then, maybe ten minutes of breath-catching weeping. My wet face cooled in the wind. Finally, I quieted. That was sixty years ago, my moment. I believe I was feeling, for the first time, the pulse of love in my own body and in the world.

My life, as I know it, began in the fertile emptiness following that dam-break of tears. I have accepted much. Now, I await that other voice, not mine, to whisper, *You are accepted.* That grace which finds us of its own accord.

The moment when the foul ball rolls up to my feet and is declared fair.

The Heartbeat of Ordinary Things

Another gray February morning,
I try to feed myself back
to life here in the living room.
Food has become rock, paper, scissors.
The bright emptiness at the center
of my coat-rack body buoys,
lifts me from the floor as if one day
I might rise and hang suspended,
hovering like a hummingbird.

The only thing I can do now
is go down into the basement
and pray for everybody.
Kerouac's words, before he coughed up
his life in his mother's toilet,
her little bungalow, 10th Avenue North,
St. Petersburg, Florida.
I have been to that house.
There is no basement.
Beneath my living room,
there is a basement.
Below that I don't know what.

I do pray, but not for everybody.
I wouldn't know how.
The Lord's Prayer; The Three Refuges:
in the Buddhas, the Dharma and the Sangha;
The Three Determinations: Let the mind
rest on the Dharma; the Dharma rest on Poverty;
Poverty rest on Death. Then, my own small
string of words: *Bless me; Teach me;*
Protect me this day.
I make the sign of the cross,
in my mind, in my speech, in my heart.

I do not want much for myself anymore.
I do not fear pain. I know it will cease.
I will miss the world, the heartbeat
of ordinary things, those I love,
those who love me.
Bless me with no memory of this life.
I do not wish to return.

When I say these words,
in prayer, I have no sense
they are being heard; nor that they travel far.
It is more like the common work
of cleaning a window after sunset
or sweeping a sidewalk bare of dead leaves.
Then, I watch and rest my heart
in the patient and faithful trees
held in place by the sky,
each breath a life of its own.

There are photographs, posted from top to bottom
on the refrigerator door, a kitchen album,
a mural of faces watching over me.
My father Dan Ragain kneels on the pier,
back home in Illinois.
He holds a stringer of bluegill,
his arms spread wide, a necklace of jewels.
March, 1978. He would have been sixty-two.
He is not smiling. The surface of the Polaroid is cracked
like a mirror. Beneath the photo
I have written, *the nerves run in all directions.*
Each time I leave the house,
I kiss the tip of my finger and touch his face.
The image of his face. He was fed
to a crematorium in St. Petersburg, Florida.
What is it that remains?

And a photo of Daniel Thompson, dear brother,
preaching rain in a dry season.
And Virginia Dunn, dear sister, washing

the feet of the new dead.
Yesterday, I noticed, for the first time,
that those years of fingertip-pressed kisses
have begun to darken and wear away their faces.

May it be my fate, my way out of here,
to be worn away by kisses, to be rubbed out,
then sent on my journey across
the flowering desert, abloom after a cool spring rain.

When I do fade like smoke, surrendered
kisses will be returned to their rightful owners.

If you later find a photo taped to a page,
an image of my face,
do what I would do for you,
kiss the tip of your finger and touch my face.
Press hard till the heartbeat pulses in your fingertip.
Wherever I am, I will look up.

Trust that the whorled print will later guide you
through the maze of the underworld.

What you do now will serve you later.
Do it again and again till that map lives in memory.

Do not fail to make your secret plans now
while you still have breath.

Maj Ragain was born into a small, southeastern Illinois farm town. Home-tutored and raised on Vernor Lake, he earned a BA in English at Eastern Illinois University, and an MA in English at the University of Illinois. He has been on faculty, off and on, at Kent State University since 1969, where he obtained his PhD in 1990. He is the author of seven chapbooks of poetry and five book-length collections, all of which contribute to *Clouds Pile Up in the North: New & Selected Poems.* In 2004, Verde Gallery of Champaign, Illinois, presented "Vision to Verse/Verse to Vision: A Visual and Poetic Dialogue," featuring poetry by Maj Ragain and paintings by Jessica Damen. Maj has served for more than thirty years as host to open poetry readings in Kent, currently at Last Exit Books, monthly, downtown. Poetry continues to build and walk that bridge between solitude and community. These poems are dedicated to the Kent community who midwifed them onto the page.

Cover artist Jessica Damen is a painter, mother, grandmother, and wife. She has also been called the "Lewis Carroll of Baltimore" by artist Grace Hartigan, who said that her paintings, "Like William James . . . [have] a gift for psychology in her depiction of children . . . [And] her use of paint is both sensual and tough."

Maj Ragain's sensual and tough poems have inspired Damen since they met while resident fellows at the Fine Arts Work Center in Provincetown, Massachusetts.

Damen received an MFA from the Maryland Institute College of Art (MICA), Hoffberger Graduate School of Painting. She has received prizes and resident fellowships from museum curators. Her works can be found in private and public collections.